JENN
KEEP MAKING
YOUR DIFFERENCE
AND KEEP ON

Choosing Your Power

all the best
Wade Paul
April '13

Choosing Your Power

BECOMING WHO YOU DESERVE TO BE, AT HOME AND IN THE WORLD!

DR WAYNE D PERNELL

BALBOA
PRESS

A DIVISION OF HAY HOUSE

ISBN: 978-1-4525-6455-5 (sc)
ISBN: 978-1-4525-6457-9 (hc)
ISBN: 978-1-4525-6456-2 (e)

Library of Congress Control Number: 2013900093

Balboa Press books may be ordered through booksellers or by contacting:

Balboa Press
A Division of Hay House
1663 Liberty Drive
Bloomington, IN 47403
www.balboapress.com
1-(877) 407-4847

Printed in the United States of America

Balboa Press rev. date: 01/07/2013

For my mom, Beverly Pernell, who taught,
loved, gave, and supported. And then supported
and loved and gave some more. With all my
love back to you, I know you can feel it.

Contents

Preface

With gratitude and awe, I salute you on your journey to this point and as you pick up and embark on your next journey to engage in Choosing Your Power! I salute you because I'm taking this path with you, and I know the difficulties and the triumphs we will continue to encounter along the way.

This book began with my thoughts over the past couple of decades. I had in mind the working title of *A Worthy Struggle*. As humans in the world, we all encounter struggles we need to get over or through. Sometimes just getting up and sorting through all the necessary to-do items every day brings us can be a struggle. From managing relationships to finances, spirit to family, the struggle of being human really is a worthy struggle.

As I wrote, I realized that my focus on the struggle wasn't helpful. I seemed to be celebrating the struggle and working against my intent: getting through it. So I turned my focus to what I wanted to share instead of what I wanted to put behind me. Instead of the struggles we encounter in daily life, I wanted to bring to life and share the steps necessary for you to become who you deserve to be and embrace the process of Choosing Your Power.

And from there the title of this book, *Choosing Your Power*, took me on a path of putting into words the lessons that will help you find your missing peace. As a transformational leader, I guide people in getting unstuck, truly becoming who they deserve to be in the world, and living their lives fulfilled—authentically, powerfully, and productively. With pleasure and deepest gratitude for allowing me into your life, I invite you to journey forth into the pages of this book as you begin Choosing Your Power!

You're invited to join me at www.ChoosingYourPower.com where you'll receive free downloads and other information and offers to help you on your journey of **Choosing Your Power!**

ACKNOWLEDGMENTS

A voice, my voice, buried deep inside found encouragement to come to life in the world and onto these pages as Shannon, my wife, offered support that included kind words and the gift of time. For those gifts and so much more, I am grateful.

My father, Dr. Godfrey Pernell, also motivated my writing. At over ninety years old, he continues to inspire, cajole, and encourage others to actively engage in learning, take from the smorgasbord of life, and "do good stuff."

Tami Osmer Glatz, my buddy from college, brought fluidity to my words in her ability to read, edit, and suggest bridges to thoughts where I knew what I meant but the reader might not, not having my inner map.

Huge acknowledgment spills from me for my original fan club: Jacob, Lucas, Daniella, Sarina, and Trinity, who watched me in wonder, laughed at my jokes, and now take on their own very individual journeys. Whether or not they know it, each serves as inspiration to drive me forward. I proudly stand in awe as I watch them engaging in the world and choosing their power.

The team at Balboa Press deserves accolades, as well. Each of them has shared his or her areas of strength and I have learned a lot along the way. It is an honor to have a great group of people guiding the way.

And to you, my reader, who makes this work important. I write so that you'll find essential steps to help yourself and people you encounter as you test what it's like to begin Choosing Your Power. Your journey matters and makes a difference. Share what you learn, stay strong, and stay soft. Yes, I acknowledge *you*.

INTRODUCTION

So many people have struggled with finding their personal voices as they seek validation for their existence from others. They come face-to-face with questions of "Am I good enough?" and "Why can't people just get along with me?" and "There's more to my life than this, right?" Well, yes. And you're holding this book because you matter! You matter! You know it, and you're looking for ways to expand your relationships at home and at work and feel rewarded in both.

Choosing Your Power is a book for those who don't want to feel stuck anymore, those who know there is more to life than they've lived so far, and those who want to continue to give and feel rewarded and fulfilled in doing so. This book is written as your guide to living life more fulfilled—authentically, powerfully, and productively.

Think about how you awaken in the morning. It's possible you're not terribly excited to roll out of bed. In fact, some days you get up because you have to, not because you want to. Picture yourself getting up: your jaw is relaxed and not tense, and you're looking forward to what you can create in your day, not in fending off the day's demands. It's a different start, and it can be the way you begin your day. The way you start your morning sets the tone for the day. Are you rushed and anxious or relaxed and eager? Take a moment to picture what that might look like for you. Yes, it really is possible.

This book is a labor of love based in vulnerability and pure heart. It began as a book designed to help people get over the struggles in their daily lives. It evolved into a book that you can use as a guide to live your life truly fulfilled. You'll work on self-improvement, your relationships, and your leadership style. (Yes, if you're watched by anyone from kids to coworkers, you're a leader. So let's look at your style, shall we?) You will learn ways to feel stronger, much stronger. For with that vulnerability of looking within comes true strength and the ability to live authentically. You'll choose what you pack in your bags carefully as we embark on a journey of discovery together. Here, I'll invite you to join me on a journey of letting go of the struggles of the past, embracing the challenges of the day, and looking ahead at how every day you take on Choosing Your Power.

Trust me to expertly guide you to examine your life and lead you to learn from your successes and challenges. I'll help you enter a place of understanding where you now take into account how you got here. You'll reflect on what you're thinking, feeling, or creating and celebrate those things as you move forward to actually become an even more powerful, productive, and authentic *you*.

Remember, you are human, and it's okay to have been stuck; just don't stay there. Learn. Take what has been useful in the past and build a better future that's positive and bright with new skills and better support—a future that starts *now*.

You're pretty good now. I mean, you survived to this point, right? Still, you know there's more out there. This will help. Really. As you take this book with you, you're giving a gift to yourself (and potentially to someone else as well). The words on the pages that follow are for you. I'm proud of them and what they can do for you. Though I haven't written this book as a workbook or a guide, I have included a few worksheets for you to use because there are a few exercises for you to do sometime and certainly some steps to follow. That said, I've written this book as if you were sitting with me. Consider this a conversation over tea with me. Enjoy taking the time to reflect on the concepts as you determine where and how you can immediately apply them in your life.

The title of this book is no accident. If you chose to italicize any one of the three words, Choosing Your Power, you'd notice that *choosing* is active and powerful in itself. You'd see that the choice is no one else's but truly *yours*. You'd also find that *power* comes in so many forms; whether the energy that comes through you is healing, creative, or directive, you get to stand up and be seen in the world for who you truly are, authentically.

So take a step and get started. You know what life is like without exploring these concepts. Practice just one new concept today and see what happens. Then find me online at www.Facebook.com/WaynePernell and let me know what you think.

Also, be sure to head to my website where you can be the first to learn about new offerings and free downloads at www.ChoosingYourPower.com.

Break through your struggles and make strides every single moment as you engage in *Choosing Your Power*.

CHAPTER 1

Stop Thinking

STOP THINKING.

1

Chapter 2

If You'd Just …

You're about to build on the strengths you have and learn some new tools to begin Choosing Your Power. That's what this book is about. It's a journey of exploration and stepping into the self you deserve to be.

In this chapter, I invite you to *stay curious*. I'm going to help you reframe some of the "simple" rules of success. It's about being curious rather than petulant. You know, like an adolescent who does the opposite of what he or she is told. You can be skeptical. Just allow yourself to look at all the potential sides of something. And in terms of petulance, well, it's easy to get fed up with the "if you'd just have a positive attitude" stuff. So engage in a sense of wonder, stay curious, and come with me …

As intended by the directive from chapter 1, it's important to slow down enough to be with yourself for a second. Quiet your mind. Judgment comes quickly. So stop thinking. Stop judging. And stop listening to the stuff that translates to "If you would just _____, your life would be oh so much better." There's no *just* about anything you do.

You know the fill-in-the-blank stuff I'm talking about:

» If you'd just believe in yourself …

» If you'd just try harder …

» If you'd just have a better attitude …

If is so powerful, and I'll guide you to daring to desire in a few chapters. For now, we'll look at the not-so-pleasant side of things. Yes, I have to take you here. You're a little cynical anyway, so this shouldn't be too terrible for you.

Being told that things could be better if … is a tough thing. You've heard it before; you've told it to yourself before; and you even want to think it's true. You might even do the thing that you believe would make your life better if you could. But it's like being told to stay warm when you don't have a jacket. You'd love to put it on. But really? How do you just have a better attitude or just believe in yourself when you never have? You can fly! How do you guide yourself down a path of success if you've never been taught how? Oh, and *just* have a positive attitude, and it'll work itself out. Really? It'll work itself out? Well, it would if ... but there you go again with that not-so-positive attitude. Why should it work out if you're not going to be positive to start with?

What really comes first, success or the positive attitude? Having a better attitude and truly believing in yourself aren't the places you start. You get there, so let's start with where you are. You got to where you are by having the tools (or strategies or instincts or dumb luck) to get there. The point is that *something* is working.

Don't "yeah but" that concept here. You might be a total wreck right now, or you might be the most successful person on the planet. Either way, you're here, and either way, you can choose to improve. We all can. The point is that no matter what your life situation is right now, something is working so that you are alive and willing to consider improving. *That* is what's working for you. You're considering getting better; you've begun to accept that things can be different, and you've entertained how you can continue Choosing Your Power!

CELEBRATION POINTS:

1. You have tools. They've worked to get you to where you are now. That's a place somewhere above mere survival. Congratulations!

2. You're considering getting better, and you're wondering how to do that. That's fantastic because when you wonder *how*, you're asking a question that will help you sharpen the tools

you already have. Asking better questions gets you better answers. Keep asking!

3. You're willing to consider additional tools. You're not quite sure what you have, and you may not be certain about what you need. That's confusing enough *and* it's worthy of celebration.

Congratulations! Really. A lot of people don't even think about getting better. You are on track simply by wondering! Remember that "stay curious" thing. That puts you ahead of the game already!

START WITH AN INVENTORY.

Look around you. Look in the mirror. Yeah, go ahead ... Just ignore those not-so-kind thoughts. Reflect on your friendships. Who in your life has made a really positive impact on you? Okay, now for the harder part. You're holding this book because there are also people in your life who have made not-so-positive impacts on you. You can take a moment to reflect on them as well. They've helped you become who you are right now.

ACKNOWLEDGE WHAT YOU HAVE THAT'S WORKING.

Take a minute now. Seriously, just reflect on—truly think about—the top six things that are working for you. You have them. It could be the fact that you're thinking about it, it could be that you're talking back to these words and ready to argue with me that not a whole lot is working, or it could be the fact that you've actually got a list of things that *are* working. So stop the chatter and get a clear list. What are the top six things in your life that are working for you?

Now take a few minutes to break from reading, just long enough to stop the chatter and look for the positive. One more time. Really. Do this now.

ACKNOWLEDGE WHAT YOU HAVE THAT'S NOT WORKING.

Wow. It seems like humans get trained to look at the not so great. We can walk into the most beautiful halls, museums, and cathedrals with shrines painted in gold and trimmed in precious gems and surrounded by dazzling stained glass, and you know what? Our eyes will catch on the one tile that is missing way up in the far corner. It's so easy to go to the "this is what's wrong" place.

Think about people who live their lives only focusing on the "what's wrong." They find it, and instead of simply noticing, they'll latch onto what's wrong and become slightly superior for finding it. They might even use the fact that they found the "wrong" thing as leverage to be offended. "You said *this* and it happened *that* way." That's a trap, and while it feels better in the moment, if you've gone to that superior place or if you're judging something as being less than or wrong, you're only serving to push other people or significant experiences away.

Don't.

As an exercise—and as an exercise *only*—let's indulge that part of you. Let's go to the place where you can look at "what's wrong" and focus on what's not working or what needs fixing in your life. Move from examining what's wrong to what you need as a solution. Remember, this chapter's title is "If You'd Just ..." So, let's explore the sense of that—the "if only" feeling. What's wrong, and what needs fixing?

» Do you need a different job?

» Do you need a different partner or for your family to be different somehow?

» Do you need more money?

» Do you need more friends?

» Do you need a different home or living situation?

» Do you need a different car, computer, or cell phone?

In chapter 7, we'll dive into a list of "Watch Words." There, we will explore how oppressive the word *need* really is. It's time to reframe any of what's missing in your life and look at two things. First, stop playing the victim in the world and living at the whim of others. Start by changing the word *need* to the word *want*. In Chapter 5 we'll discuss how to move from desire to destination. For now, just know that you can be back in control if you claim a true desire over a need. Notice also, that being clear about your desire(s) is different than merely floating out an empty wish.

> » I want a job where my talents are noticed and I'm respected/valued for my contributions (vs. I *wish* I could run this place).

> » I want a partner who supports me and challenges me enough to grow (vs. I want a wealthy, good looking partner to just take care of me).

> » I want a car that is reliable (vs. I *wish* I had a Maserati).

Second, acknowledge that you have tools and strengths and that you're not done yet.

> » I got to this age by using the tools I had.

> » I'm still learning, and every day offers exciting opportunities.

> » I picked up this book because I believe in myself, and I truly want to grow in positive ways.

So the to-do action steps you get to begin to practice are:

1. Become attuned to the language you use as you speak with others and, perhaps more important, when you speak with yourself. Beware of using the word *need* when thinking about things you want to attract to yourself and be conscious of

even the small things like ordering food ("I need a ..." vs. "I'd like a ...").

2. Interrupt any language that contains judgment or condemnation (about yourself, any part of yourself, or others). As you talk, you may hear yourself use language that might tear you or others down, even if only a little.

   a. By not participating in gossip or judging yourself negatively, you train your mind and create openings for the much more positive to get in.

   b. Body image and body size actually change when you start focusing on facets you *like* rather than focusing on those you don't like or that you worry about. Do you like your hands, your calves, or your toes? Focus there anytime you feel like you need to comment on the way your jeans fit or any other attribute that isn't quite "right."

3. Build your menu of alternate words so you can change the language you use. Stop yourself midsentence and shift your focus to something more positive.

Words become powerful. You say them to yourself, you hear them from others, and the problem is that you begin to believe them. The point here, and in fact all along the way, is *choice*. Truly choose what you focus on and don't just become lazy by leaping to conclusions or making assumptions. That means start to look at the information you have differently. You have information to which you ascribe a certain feeling or impart power. Examine; don't assume.

It's clear that making assumptions often gets people into trouble. There is, however, one assumption that can set you just a bit freer: *no one woke up this morning to make your life miserable.* It's not raining to make you wet. The flight wasn't late to make you worry about your connection or your meeting. It's not being done *to* you. Whatever it is, it just exists. It's information for you, and it's neutral.

All information is neutral. Even if you were told you won the lottery, that's neutral information. Most people would see it as a fairly positive thing. A few might view it as not so great. The thing is it starts as neutral. It's a condition to which you get to choose to react.

All of life is exactly that—a condition to which you get to choose to react. So starting by bargaining with yourself or the powers that be with words like *if you'd just* makes no sense. It neither supports you nor empowers you to get further. You can choose though.

You can choose what you think by interrupting what you were thinking. After practicing choosing your words and selecting what you think, you actually begin to choose *how* you think. Since your thoughts affect everything you have and bring into your life, choosing the positive makes a big difference.

So stop thinking. Reflect on what has been working and what has brought the positive into your life. Interrupt what hasn't been working, and begin to substitute the positive.

As an exercise (yes, another one), describe your clothes. Writing down the description makes this exercise that much more potent. Or say it out loud. If you're in public, it's okay to whisper. Describe what you're wearing. The task isn't just to list your clothes. Rather it's to deliberately create a *neutral* inventory. There's no such thing as "I'm wearing my old faded top" or, on the other side of judgment, "I've got on my really nice slacks." Instead, go deliberately neutral: "I'm wearing a pale blue knit top, dark blue pressed jeans, and brown open-toe sandals." There's no mention of what brand or how nice or beaten up they are. They just exist.

The purpose of this exercise is to practice finding the neutral space and then *choosing* to impart a positive impression on what you're noticing. Let's say your top is old and faded. Calling it pale blue instead of saying it used to be cobalt is the task. Then when you come to this next step, say something nice about it. "This pale blue top has lasted through three years of regular wear and washing." That's so different than "Ugh, this old thing!"

Now let's try it for other situations. Describe your surroundings. Go neutral and then find something positive: "My apartment is so small and cluttered" turns into "I have a place to live and many of my things are visible" which then turns to "I love having a space to call my own with the ability to keep my stuff with me."

Practice the following statements:

» I work with some interesting people. I'm glad I can choose to act differently than they do when faced with stressors.

» I'm on the road with some expressive people. I can choose to smile, knowing that clenching my jaw doesn't get me there any faster. These people are good reminders for me, and if I could, I'd like to thank them for helping me smile.

» I've just finished reading the second chapter in this book, and I'm already taking steps to change my life for the better. I'm practicing new ways of thinking. By acknowledging my progress, I can choose to let go of past patterns and welcome opportunities to find new ways of being. This feels good!

CHAPTER 3

Permission Granted

YOU'RE SORRY, AND I'M CONFUSED.

STAND IN A BUILDING'S LOBBY, waiting to enter the elevator. As the doors open and the stream of people flows out, some people push past while others tiptoe by, squeaking out apologies. "Oh, sorry."

Yep, you're sorry, and I'm confused.

I don't quite understand what happened that caused you to apologize for exiting the elevator and making room for me to step in. Really, I don't get it. Chances are you don't understand it either. It's just what you do. In fact, you probably didn't even know you were doing it.

It's time to break away from being apologetic and step into being who you really, truly are: powerful and valuable in the world. Really, what exactly are you apologizing for? You're sorry that you're in *my* way? Don't we both belong here? Is it possible that you're sorry for taking up any space in the world at all?

You know who I'm talking about. The chronic apologizers. It's a disease. It has to be. It's a disease in the world that an apology is the go-to standard way to respond.

There are some people who seem to apologize more frequently; women are probably just more vocal about it. I know there are men who apologize for just breathing another person's air too. You may recognize yourself; if it's you, you're likely to want to apologize for having apologized. And if it's not you, it's likely you know someone who takes care of everyone else so that no waves are ever made.

Far too often I come across people who catch themselves doing something for which they feel compelled to apologize. The apology, "Oh, sorry," speaks volumes. True remorse and regret can be conveyed appropriately in the sorry remark. But that's not always how it's used. Often it's a tool of survival.

"Sorry" is used to preempt the negative judgment that comes after being caught doing something perceived as wrong. It's almost as if the "guilty" person is saying, "If I apologize before you have a chance to get mad at me for being in the wrong place at the wrong time or for doing something wrong, then you won't be as mad at me." If others can't get mad, then they can't punish you. So you'll cower and punish yourself first. This fear-based response helps very little in the long run. Most people don't like to be judged. Some people hold a significant amount of fear about thinking someone might think badly of them, so they shrink back, apologize, and do what they can to placate and make nice, even when no real offense exists.

That may have worked to get you through day-to-day survival of an abusive, alcoholic, or otherwise oppressive household as a child. We each have tools that have helped us grow up. The task now is to really assess whether the tools we have been using to get here are still serving us. As adults, we owe it to ourselves and to the people around us—at home, at work, and beyond—to show up. So now that we are adults, "sorry" is a very, very broken tool. From whom are you protecting yourself?

Think about how you are judging yourself and then how you train others to judge you. You teach others how to treat you by how you present yourself to the world. As noted in the introduction of this book, Choosing Your Power is about accepting and then overcoming your own worthy struggle. How have you judged yourself? How have you presented yourself to the world? How have you allowed others to treat you? How have you been training others to treat you?

Now that you're thinking about those things—on the path to Choosing Your Power—ask yourself how you would rather be treated.

Did you know you had a choice?

What path do you really want to create? There are harder questions you can put off for a little while but not for too much longer: *How do I value myself in the world? What do I really desire and, dare I ask, even deserve?*

Ask yourself whether you deserve from others the disdain you seem to cast upon yourself. You know you deserve better. You know deep down that you're better than that. Don't you dare insert a "yeah but" here. You know you deserve love and life and breathing and vacations and on and on, including the same things other people get to enjoy without apologies or excuses.

Not only do you deserve, but you're entitled. What a word, eh? You are entitled to enjoy life. So from the most positive sense of the word and not the bratty sense of entitlement, you need to be able to stand up and ask for—or even take—what you deserve to have. People won't give to you the things you only dream or wish about. You have to move from desire to destination by taking action, and you get to practice doing it without apologizing.

As suggested in the previous chapter, you can practice interrupting negative thoughts. At this point you can smile about it. It's happening; you're recognizing it. It may even be starting to feel absurd, and that should give you something else to smile about. I'd call that movement and growth. Congratulations because this feeling badly for being judged as "bad" or "wrong" shows up in some funny places.

While staying at a hotel not long ago, I happened across a young woman, another guest of the hotel, who had found the maid's cart in a storage room that had been left open. She was taking packets of coffee so she'd have some for the next morning. I passed the storage room on the way to my room. The woman looked up and furtively put the coffee away, saying, "Sorry, I was getting coffee for the morning." I looked at her, confused about what she had said. "You don't have to apologize to *me*," I said. "I did the same thing earlier." When did I become the coffee police? If you need something and can take action to get it, why not simply ask for it or get it yourself?

When you've excused your behavior with an apology, you've asked for the approval of someone. "Sure. No problem. Go ahead. It's okay." Choose those words for the voices in your head to echo to you. "I belong here" is a really good place to start.

As an exercise, reflect back on the times you've said, "Oh, sorry," when you meant, "Hey, I'm doing something for myself." What comes up for you as you reflect back? The question is this: How much of yourself are you willing to give away because you don't know whether you belong or because you could be judged badly for being seen doing something for yourself? Are you allowed to get off of an elevator without apologizing for being on it? Are you allowed to get coffee for yourself because it's just easier than calling the front desk person, who would then contact housekeeping, who would interrupt you just to bring you a packet? Are you entitled to make that call to get that end result? *Yes!* Is it easier sometimes to take care of what you need in the moment, and are you entitled to do that? Yes and *yes!*

Think about other habits and opportunities. At the grocery store, begin to observe how others interact. While some move forward, others apologize. Personally, my habit is to offer a word of gratitude. My thank-you really means, "Thanks for stopping your cart for me so I could get by you." That's so different from "So sorry I was in your way."

The next time you're shopping, be aware of others around you. This chapter isn't a license to be rude. It's a push to awaken the part of you that goes along to get along, and it's a push to get you to start questioning whether that's the best place to spend your energy. Certainly there are times when the word *sorry* is appropriate. You can feel empathy for another person's dilemma and be sorry that he or she is experiencing something unpleasant. You might have accidentally caused harm to someone in some way. In these cases, feeling sorry really *is* appropriate. In fact, having empathy is highly correlated with success in the world. However, there's a difference between having empathy and placating. So saying you're sorry isn't something that needs to disappear entirely; just don't live there.

Sometimes apologies serve to assuage the anger of others. They calm a conflict, so chronic apologizers tend to use the language of apology preemptively. They'll apologize to keep the calm and not make waves. Conflict isn't tolerable to those caught in the apology loop, so it's better to apologize than to let someone become angry. The thing is the expected conflict probably didn't even exist in the first place. You have permission, as an adult, to be who you are. You don't need permission—not mine, not anyone's. Really. *Really!*

Just be. Simply ... *be.*

Focus on personal growth. No longer going along to get along, you'll need to be aware of the choices you're making at every turn and allow yourself the opportunity to be all right about being in an aisle with your shopping cart, picking a place to sit in a public venue (like a park, classroom, public transport vehicle, or movie theater), or getting in or out of an elevator.

You'll also need to decide when it's okay to have a voice. Better still, take a look at when it's not okay. It's almost never not okay; without the double negative, that means it's pretty much always okay! You know you *deserve* to be seen and heard! Look out! Here comes that *entitled* word again. You are entitled to your voice, your opinion, your wants, your dreams, and your desires. It's a common experience for people who have grown up as givers and peacemakers to shut themselves down and go silent instead of expressing an opinion. Peacemakers so seldom get what they want because they've given themselves away for the sake of *not* making waves. They then sit by, hoping to be noticed for all they've given, which of course doesn't happen. That breeds resentment and internal conflict. Going along to get along almost never brings the result you truly desire.

Dwelling in the land of sorry can actually lead to a depression. The ugly cycle is that the more you say you are sorry, the sorrier you'll feel. The sorrier you feel, the less of *you* that shows up as worthy in the world. The less of you that shows up as worthy in the world, the sorrier you'll become.

You have permission to be in the world without apology. You have permission to have an opinion, and you have permission for your opinion to be different than other people's opinions. Think about it; do you ever allow yourself the opportunity to be right? Look at the roles you've played in your life—as a family member growing up, as a family member now. Look at yourself as an individual. *Can you be right and allow others to be right also?* That is, just because someone has a strong opinion, there can be (and always is) more than one way to view any situation.

What this means is that you don't ever have to give yourself away because someone else demands to be more right than you. You have a choice about how you verbalize your thoughts. The key here is to know that you have permission to have your own opinion and wants and dreams and desires. The other key is that you have a choice.

When you apologize as a means to not make waves, the worthy, valuable you is lost to the unworthy, depressed, immobile placating automaton. Permission is granted to show up and be strong!

Try this exercise. You can do it alone, but it's more fun to do with a friend. With a stopwatch or a countdown timer, set twenty seconds as a marker. For twenty seconds say out loud the following phrases and/or something like them in any order: "Oh, sorry. Really sorry. I didn't mean to. Sorry. Oh, uh, excuse me. I'm sorry." Repeat that for twenty seconds total. If you're doing this exercise with a friend, both of you should start by facing each other and leaning in and then back without touching, as if you are trying to get by each other. At the same time, speaking over each other, both of you should say the phrases, as many of them as you can, repeating the "I'm sorry" stuff for twenty seconds.

Did you do it? If you did, you found out some things. If you didn't yet, then I encourage you to do the exercise. You'll find out that it's pretty absurd, and you might even end up laughing at how absurd it is. It takes a lot of energy to apologize that much. And twenty seconds seems like a long time because apologizing for nothing is really hard work. It's energy intensive and a waste. Gosh, this seems like the perfect thing to cut out of your life! Think about it. How much of your life have you wasted by being sorry for something that wasn't yours to be sorry for? Yikes! Absurd! Now that's something to smile at! Not that you've wasted time but rather that you've gotten a sense of something worth eliminating to create room for the more positive.

Which leads us to the second exercise. The setup conditions are the same: set the stop watch or countdown timer for twenty seconds, and with a partner or alone, you'll say some stronger words out loud. Take a firm footing. Even put your hands on your hips. If you're with a partner, you can firmly shake his or her hand. Say the following: "I'm glad to be here. I belong here. I'm happy I'm here. I'm happy you're here. It's great to *be*. It's great to be here and seen and to see you. I'm happy to be here.

I belong here." As before, you don't have to read that as a script. Use those words in any order, adding any positive thoughts congruent with affirming your presence.

After twenty seconds, you may notice that it felt good to do that. It felt good, *and* it was fun! You're laughing and breathing and smiling, not out of embarrassment but out of empowerment. You might also notice that where twenty seconds during the first exercise seemed long, these twenty seconds flew! You were just getting started. And so it is; you are just getting started. You deserve to be here. You deserve to *be*.

What you need is an *apologectomy*. By removing the "apology gland," you'll be able to live a healthier life. There'll be no more sorry-itis (inflammation of the "sorry"). You'll be left with a sense of a right to belong. Take a breath, roll your shoulders back so that your chest opens a bit, and look up. Open your arms like you are accepting the applause of the world and (as strange as this all seems, give it a chance) say out loud, "I am valuable, and I have a valuable gift to share." Practice that. Just reading it won't help you. Take a chance on practicing something new in your life. Go back over those last few sentences. Let go of being sorry and apologizing for being in the world. Dare to be big, even if just for an instant. Try it on and see how it feels.

While the title of this chapter is "Permission Granted," you've learned about how people look for approval and forestall judgment. You can now see that apologizing is a means by which to disarm or diffuse. It is a tool that worked to get you out of childhood to where you are now.

The thing is you're bigger than that, and you don't need it anymore. You're bigger than that person who used to apologize at every turn. You have a right to be in the world. You belong.

Are you allowed to be Choosing Your Power?

Yes, permission granted!

CHAPTER 4

Not Good Enough

STOP PRETENDING YOU'RE NOT AN IMPOSTER.

OR ...

STOP PRETENDING. YOU'RE NOT AN IMPOSTER!

YOUR PERSONAL PUNCTUATION MAKES ALL the difference in your approach to—and the response from—the world. At some point, we each feel caught by the sense that maybe, just maybe, we don't know enough and therefore aren't good enough to be doing what we're doing. There's a looming sense of judgment that we project onto others. That is, we judge ourselves in the harshest fashion that we *imagine* others might judge us. It's almost always negative, of course.

So the challenge is to face the harsh questions head-on. What if you were found out for all that you truly *don't* know? There you are pretending to be somebody, an expert of sorts, and you worry, wondering who knows about the "real" you. What if someone finds out that you don't know everything? When faced with the hidden judgment behind these questions, we tend to shrink a little inside. We get a little quieter, and we see that someone louder who seems to know the truth has offered us both relief and inner humiliation. By simply speaking up, that person has validated our fears: We really don't know enough. We really aren't good enough.

So starts a downward spiral. We could get caught in it and seek evidence of further "not knowing" and essentially being not good enough for this group in which we've found ourselves. We could seek people who have lesser standards or levels of expectation and become a hero. Or we could snap out of it and recognize that each of us has a strong knowledge base and that by voicing an opinion or a direction, we step into a leadership role with accountability. By doing that, we force ourselves to be better. By recognizing that maybe you don't know it *all* now, you push yourself to know more.

Truthfully, you'll never know it all. Even the foremost experts in the world never stop learning. Maybe that's what makes them experts! Seeking to be better *is* good enough. Having a voice and an opinion *is* good enough. When we let doubt stir, we wonder, *What if I'm not good enough?* There is a better question. *What if I am?*

What if you *are* good enough? Now there's an awesome burden!

Really, it's so easy to go to that place of fear of being wrong or being found out for being an imposter. What's funny in a sad sort of way is that everyone feels that from time to time. Anyone who has ever been in charge of doing something has had at least a fleeting sense of "Who am I to be doing this?" That's normal and reasonable, unless you get stuck there. Then it stops being either normal or reasonable. So you must just keep going.

Rely on the adage of "fake it till you make it," and keep going. The true changes that take you from where you are to where you want to be lie in the actions you take—and repeat—every day. So who are you to be doing this, to be daring to dream of doing something different? Well … who are you *not* to?

People get stuck asking themselves, "Who am I to be the one to want to show up in a certain way?" Everyone has a dream. Some people have trained themselves not to dream big anymore; that said, everyone has a dream.

Fear stops people from pursuing their dreams. They question themselves about what they know and convince themselves about all they don't know. Stop looking for evidence of not knowing enough, and for the sake of practice, begin looking at ways your gift is unique.

There's also the responsibility of being the one with the gift and having to show up with it. What if you *are* good enough? Fear stops people from pursuing what they hope to be possible because they wonder who will judge them for daring to dream and how they will be perceived for having a voice. This is especially true if daring to share your voice, your opinions, or your presence is new to you. Others know you for your history. You may never have been like this in the past. But the past doesn't dictate the future. It only defines how you got to this point. So what's your next step? Choose!

Choose? What if it's the "wrong" choice? What if the direction you choose isn't the right direction? You can make an active choice to sit idly by while the world keeps moving, or you can engage with the world at whatever level you're at. Paralysis of thought can lead to true depression as one gives up the fire and light he or she once held in pursuing his or her own unique "thing." Can you imagine if our historical figures—great artists, scientists, musicians, and writers—had gotten stuck wondering if what they had to offer was good enough?

So what if you aren't good enough for a particular thing *right now*. Does your current state dictate your potential? No. You know it doesn't. Neither does the thought that you're not good enough for *something* mean that you're not good enough for *everything*. So flip your thinking a hundred and eighty degrees and look at your situation from the other side. What *are* you good at?

Are you *good enough* at anything? Can you say it out loud? "I'm reasonably good at _____." Write that down. Get a scrap of paper, your journal, or just scratch it into the margin of this book: *I'm good enough at _____.* Then keep the thought going. *Not only am I good enough, in fact, I'm pretty darn good at it.* If you can look at anything you do and have confidence in making a claim, it builds your competence in the actual doing of it. As you see evidence of competence, your confidence builds. It becomes an upward spiral. This is something we'll delve into much more deeply in the final chapter of this book.

Confidence → Competence → Confidence

Confidence leads to the doing, which leads to an acknowledgment of competence, which leads to confidence. It then generalizes to other activities. You begin to feel yourself grow. You think to yourself, *If I'm good at this and it took practice to get there, maybe I can be good at that, knowing that it'll take practice to get there too.*

If you don't take that chance, actually risk being better, then you only rob the rest of the world of you and your gift. Instead of wondering who you are to say a certain thing or be a certain way, it's time to flip that thinking around. Let's begin by just pretending (unless you can acknowledge outright) that you have some gem hidden inside you. So if you have this special gem and it's valuable, don't others deserve to see it? Can't your share it? Look at you being selfish with your gift! What's up with that? Really? Who are you to withhold your gift—your personal special, unique gift—from the rest of the world? You *are* good enough to share who you are. Dare. Risk. Be!

When I was in graduate school, I found myself wondering about my path. Who was I to be an expert and guide others in their lives? I mean, each person has his or her own life. I found myself shrinking into a routine. It was comfortably uncomfortable. And somehow I managed to realize that I was letting my box get smaller and smaller. The routine was just that. It didn't allow for expansion. It didn't allow for anything new to enter my world. Deep down I knew that if I wanted to be better, I had to embrace my struggles, my frustration, and my comfort levels. I had to really push myself to begin choosing my own power.

Push? Push to choose to be powerful? It was actually recognizing that I needed to choose to *be power.* My routine was safe, predictable, and boring. It held me in while the world kept evolving at a scary pace. I just wanted to do my work, be judged as "good enough," get my degree, and get on with my life. I didn't want to make waves for anyone. And I certainly didn't want to upset my own little world.

And that was just it. My little world was becoming smaller because I was making it so. I was not acknowledging that I was "good enough" at the moment. Neither was I able to see that I could own the process by looking in the mirror each morning and telling myself, "Today is the day you are Choosing Your Power." I allowed the shackles of safety to hold me in. Then something smacked me. Hard.

Hit by a flare of insight, I grabbed a three by five inch index card and in bright orange ink wrote a four-letter word ending with a *k.*

I taped this word on the threshold of my bedroom door so it would be the last thing I read as I exited the safety of my room, and the boldest command stuck in my head as I entered the world. What was my reminder to myself, that four-letter word?

RISK

By reminding myself to take a risk, I was engaging in a contract with myself, one that I encourage you to do for yourself as well. The contract is simple: today, I shall do one thing different from the way I used to do it.

Whether that was to explore a different route home, try a different food for lunch, meet someone new, or simply speak up in class, my contract was to *do* something new. I wasn't going to try or attempt or wimp out. *Do* just one thing new today. Experience what it's like to *risk* breaking from your past place of comfort.

I'm not asking you to set the world on fire (not yet, anyway). I'm suggesting that you risk well. Many parents tell their kids to "be safe" as they set out on their journeys for the day. Since my insight in grad school, I've stopped wishing anyone that. Instead, my wish for others—including you, dear reader—is that you *risk well*. That doesn't mean you find the busiest intersection and step out into traffic without regard to stoplights. It means that you find something that is different from yesterday's definition of safety for your bubble and then push out from it.

Once you find yourself moving past what was, you'll begin to wonder what would have happened if you had actually begun this kind of journey sooner. As you reflect on *who* you are and *how* you are, you may find yourself wondering things like, *What have I done? What haven't I done?* Bargaining with yourself ensues. *If I had only …* And it leads you to feeling like you're not good enough. Oh hey. *Stop thinking!*

Regrets, I've had a few …

Everyone has had the feeling of shrinking, even puckering inside when they reflect back on things they *should* have changed or done differently. The feeling is self-blame: *I could have/should have said/done this thing differently. Because I didn't, it means that I'm bad/stupid/ awful.* By not doing or saying that thing differently, you've ended up feeling badly and experience negative feeling flashbacks.

Did you ever notice that we seldom have positive feeling flashbacks? No one is really ever overcome by the feeling of being great or wonderful. Wouldn't it be great to experience a sense of pleasant relaxation that is triggered by some subconscious event? Instead of feeling badly, we might have a sense of "Ahhh, when I did this thing, everyone enjoyed it so much that it just brought a wave of joy washing through me."

Right …

And why not? Why do we get stuck instead with the sense of "shoulding" on ourselves? It's because the "negative" emotions are those that stem from an internalized moral judgment. The good news is that we experience that. We care. It worries us that we might have done some harm to someone or not lived up to who we could have been in that particular moment. We become afraid of having not made the "right" choice.

It's frightening when people don't show that they have a sense of moral correctness. (And please, dear reader, there's a difference between a sense of moral rightness— knowing right from wrong—and a moral righteousness. Let go of that one.)

Moral development occurs in childhood. We learned early what was "right" and what was "wrong." We were taught by our parents, clergy members, teachers, or other adults in positions of authority. As we matured, those initial teachings guided us in our processes of growth and development. When we violate our own rules of rightness, we have that feeling of should-based judgment. When people get stuck in the *should*, the land of negative self-judgment, they have most likely failed to grow beyond their early teachings.

What most people don't recognize is that all too often, the early teachings are for younger people with limited resources to recognize that a broader scenario exists and therefore other options are possible. In short, adults tell kids how they "should" be, and kids don't have the perspective to know whether what's being imposed upon them is the right fit for them. So as we grow up, we can only make use of the lessons we've learned. It's not until we've grown up that we have a perspective that lets us look beyond those lessons and question whether they make sense. Where we get stuck is when we don't even wonder whether the lessons that kept order in the past fit our current situations.

Regrets are about self-blame and are based in judgment that isn't really current. All too often a regret starts with a sentiment of "If I knew then what I know now." In all likelihood, you didn't know what you needed to know. But you did the best you could with the resources you had. Regrets come from the giant looming "should" that's all too often unfounded.

We've all hurt people. We've hurt people we love, and at some point, we might enter into a realm of self-punishment for hurting those people. Honestly, truly, I didn't mean to hurt the people I've hurt. I don't think you've meant to hurt others either. Did you wake up today thinking about how you could best cause harm to someone? I don't think so. That's not the kind of person who would be looking at a book like this. So I'll repeat something from the last paragraph: we all did the best we could with the resources we had available to us at the time. So you have to look back at what was available to you.

Now look ahead. You have two paths to follow when you feel the gut-puckering problem of regret: atonement and forgiveness.

Atonement—can you make up for what you've done? Can you truly undo what you've done? Since you didn't set out to hurt someone, the wave of blame, shame, and regret that sweeps across you needs to be put into perspective. Others can hold you hostage for having "wronged" them. You can offer apologies (as noted in Chapter 7, the one focused on communication), and you can offer to make up for any damage done; just don't live there.

If you've broken something that can be repaired, fix it. If you've hurt someone emotionally, then apologize for the missteps you've made. The next part of the interaction is up to the other person though. It becomes his or her choice to accept your apology or hold onto it and live in the world of being offended. To hold another person hostage with guilt that is founded in being offended, though, is some of the worst kind of bullying. It's as if you're saying, "I will never let you be happy, ever, because I will continue to remind you that you offended my sensibilities." When you see it written, it looks absurd. You need to be able to be sincere in your apologies and then be able to move past the offense (and with all due diligence not repeat the earlier trespass). At that point, you cannot be responsible for how another person feels, and he or she cannot be responsible for how you feel. Holding onto the emotional baggage of another person lets neither of you grow; nor does it allow you to get better.

Atonement can take many forms. Beyond that, the next step of forgiveness is vital.

Forgiveness—difficult to achieve and vital to master, forgiveness allows for becoming unstuck from the past. Books devoted to this topic line self-help shelves. The core construct comes down to this: you may stay stuck with whatever offensive act happened to you or you committed. Or you may choose differently.

By acknowledging that an incident occurred, even a life-changing incident, you can take a snapshot of it with your mind's eye. Look at all the circumstances that led up to it and what happened during it and then recognize that you did the best you could have done in that situation. Could you have acted differently a split second sooner? Yes. You could have. For whatever reason, you didn't, and you can't go back to change that. Would acting differently have changed the outcome? That is the mystery that no one will ever be able to know.

While you can't change what happened, you can, however, build from where you are. What you did in the moment *was* good enough. Now you have choices about how to become better and more powerful in the world. Each moment becomes an opportunity for Choosing Your Power. You can choose to stay in the struggle of what was and combine that with all of the judgment that goes along with what could have been and isn't. Or you can collect your personal power, review what emerging strengths you have, and forgive yourself. Forgive the other person. Live in the present.

Depression comes from living in the past, and anxiety is at the root of living in the future. You *can* forgive yourself and others for the transgressions of the past. You *can* focus on the possible while creating a plan in the present. Release yourself from depression by forgiving yourself for the past. Look at what resources you have at your disposal now. What is available *now* ... and now ... and now? Each moment being different, you have new choices.

You have new choices, all of which are ... good enough!

These life lessons are not always the easiest, but they are the stuff you learn from the most. In the process, you become more *you*. As you let go of what once worked but no longer does, the essential you emerges strong. The real, essential, beautiful you can be compared to a sculptor's block of marble. Only by examining the lines and then chiseling away the excess "not me" can the artist make the true art object emerge. You're then left with "the real me."

But woe, the flaws! No marble sculpture is perfect. None of us are without flaws. How can this be? How can we each be "good enough" in the world if we are riddled with flaws? I'm referring to the hypercritical, awful process that people (especially women) put themselves through when they look in the mirror. I'm referring to the regrets we choose to live with. I'm referring to the times we "should" all over ourselves for not being a particular way.

The point is that you really *are* good enough exactly as you are right now. This thing called life is a journey. We're never "done," and as long as we're alive, the journey is one of discovery. From there, recognize that the greatest discovery is self-discovery. Continue on this path of discovery and look at yourself with love. Discover that you truly aren't done yet, and you'll find that you are flawed, and that's okay.

That's what I call the *Perfect Flaw*. Stop seeking perfection and recognize that you're already perfect. Perfection is *not* a set state. Perfection is an individual's critical assessment of one point in time. The judgment of perfection can and will vary from individual to individual, moment to moment.

So celebrate. You are flawed. Perfectly!

You are good enough, and with every moment you are discovering your personal power and emerging strengths. Your thoughts build you or tear you down. Because thoughts are creative energy, it's important to make each one positive. Isn't that what truly Choosing Your Power is about?

Remember that *you are good enough now*. Confidence in anything will help you feel competent. Recognizing that will, in turn, build further confidence. Risk being different than you are now! *Risk well* and grow your comfort bubble! As you do that, you can let go of holding yourself hostage to what might have been. Bargaining leads to regrets; *move on from regrets*, as they only fuel depression and keep you stuck. Acknowledge the resources you had, the actions you took, and that you would do things differently now. Then wasn't now; now is the present, and you're capable of making different choices.

Along the way, *seek progress, not perfection*. You're perfect just as you are, and that includes being perfect with the flaws you have. What you see as a flaw may be perfect for another. What others see as flaws may be perfect for you. Let go of judgment and recognize that *you're perfect now*, perfectly flawed. And all together that makes you *good enough*. Even just starting with this acknowledgment sets you well on your way to *Choosing Your Power!*

CHAPTER 5

Decisions Terminate Panic

THE "GOOD ENOUGH" QUESTIONS THAT continue to haunt us create a kind of paralysis. Do I move forward, backward, left, or right? Not knowing, we sometimes simply get stuck out of fear of making the "wrong" choice. But who judges it as wrong? Ah, well, it could be that inner critic. It could be others. Either way, the result is a fear-based inner turmoil.

We're given the opportunity to make so many mistakes that sometimes that's all we focus on. What happens if ...? What if it's wrong? Building on the information from the last chapter, you will begin to embrace the four-letter word ending in *k*, and risk ... risk being wrong. Risk being right, as well. Recognize that you have a choice. Then celebrate that you have a choice, for the ability to choose allows for the sense of control in one's life. Actually, making a choice is the act of self-empowerment.

Often the fear of facing choices can be traced back to a particular style of survival from when you were younger. There was a "right" answer that you may have been expected to have, over and over in multiple situations. Authority figures made inquiries of you, and out of fear of being punished—even if the punishment was internal embarrassment—the polar styles of either blurting out anything to get it over with or freezing in search of the "right" answer became a style preference. As one of the only tools of survival, you used it to get through. Because it worked, or at least worked well enough, as an adult you may have found yourself perpetuating that interactive style with parents, teachers, bosses, and even your chosen partner. The thing is at this point you're teaching others how to treat you because of the way you've responded in the world.

Don't let fear kill everything you know to be possible. Most people delay making difficult personal choices and end up paying a high price for doing so. We, as humans, are driven to seek pleasure and avoid pain. Look at any choice you've ever made. Do you feel like you made that choice in order to feel happier or more comfortable? Or do you feel like you "needed" to make the choice because not doing so would cause you some pain? *We get comfortable avoiding pain and end up redefining what true happiness really is.*

Out of fear of being unhappy with any particular choice or series of choices, people often find themselves living purely out of habit. That is, they live with what they know and have become comfortable with. Change is scary. Period. People fear making choices because we are afraid of any potential for unhappiness that the change might bring. Change opens people up and indeed makes us vulnerable. The saying "better the devil you know" comes from comforting those who are uncertain about making great personal changes. If others around you know who you are because of how you are, they'll encourage you to stay as you are. If your life is based on creating personal growth for yourself and encouraging growth in those around you, then change and growth become the new norm.

You can change the balance and make huge leaps in personal growth by making a single change in your reactive or responsive style. That style goes deep, and you may find yourself staring at your computer or even your refrigerator at the beginning of the day, afraid to make a choice. If you choose one thing, you have to let another go. That's an awesome responsibility and burden.

Change comes from making a decision. For so many people, though, even making that first new decision is difficult because, believe it or not, they (you) just don't know how! A prompt is sometimes necessary. You may not need to know all of the how to actually make the decision that it—whatever *it* is—is what you want!

Sometimes small things reach up and slap you right in the face. I guess I was ready for my growth spurt. It was a fortune cookie that broke me loose from my own paralyzed state. I only ever got this fortune once and have never seen it again in the hundreds of cookies I've ingested since. The fortune simply read, *Decisions Terminate Panic.*

How can it be that out of all the other cookies foretelling of travel or secret admirers, I received a nudge to be different in the world? Well, dear reader, let me pay this one forward and offer you that same nudge. I made a sign out of those words and posted it above my computer. Whenever I found myself feeling stuck and the inner turmoil rising, I'd look at that sign and simply choose. As difficult as it was, I read that clever little fortune's words and just made a decision—a choice. That left me feeling more in charge of my life—more powerful. You're now well on your way to Choosing Your Power. Keep going!

What I came to realize is that very, very seldom are we locked into decisions we make. We head down a path and have the ability to make alterations and corrections based on new information. Remember that we each do the best we can with the tools we have. It's trusting that those tools can be used that becomes difficult. Doing so allows for great personal growth.

This chapter isn't about stirring stuff up just for the heck of it. It's about recognizing that you have power in your ability to make choices. People tend to live with their unhappiness because it's easier than changing. Afraid to potentially be even unhappier or risk imposing on someone else, people allow themselves to remain stuck with what they already have. It's a hard thing to come to terms with. Still, once they are able to look at themselves and their situations and ultimately decide that they *want* to change, they begin to welcome their own power.

So rather than feeling stuck by the multitude of choices available or frozen out of fear of being wrong somehow, embrace your ability to choose freely. You may have to "go to the dark side" initially and look at the fear you've experienced. Acknowledging and understanding fear can also be empowering. Realizing that fear can be your companion whenever you are exploring unfamiliar areas in your life *can* make fear exciting. Allowing it to immobilize you is where it becomes problematic. Fear and excitement have the same physiological characteristics. If you approached a roller coaster with a friend, you might both experience elevated heart rates, a little sweat, and dilated pupils as adrenaline begins to pump. One of you might be excited and press forward, while the other might be paralyzed with fear and freeze or retreat.

As you become more aware, you'll be able to redefine your current experience in any given moment. That can make all the difference for you as you embrace life's rich experiences that follow! When faced with choices, it's so easy to find yourself focusing on the negative aspects of each possibility and then freeze, feeling as though there is no good decision. Your power comes from recognizing that you actually have a choice. From there, concentrate on the benefits of each selection available; look specifically at how each option would improve your situation.

Danger! Do *not* get stuck in "analysis paralysis." Leaders, including leaders of their own lives, need to know that two key things matter in order to become a great leader. First, get pretty darn clear about the outcome or end result you want. Second, be flexible in the way you get there. Airplanes take off on a small strip of land, fly thousands of miles, are off course 97 percent of the time, and they still land on the little strip of land that their pilots intend for them to land on. How? They're pushed off course or diverted deliberately, and still they make use of the tools they have to make appropriate course corrections along the way. Choose a destination; choose a direction. Go!

What if you don't know what you want? What if you're not really truly sure of what that strip of land is "supposed to be" when you land on it? You know what? You've been playing this game of life long enough to know what you *don't* want. Usually my advice will be to focus on the positive only. If you are really not sure what you want, then at least be clear about what you don't want. Define it and put it in a corner. Try this: take a small sheet of paper, and on the lower left side, about an inch up from the corner, draw a small box to the bottom edge of the paper about an inch over from the corner. There. That defines the space of what you don't want.

Look at it. "I don't want *that!*" If you know that where you're headed is not there, it means the rest of the world is available. See how much possibility is left? It's important to do this so you can really track what's available to you.

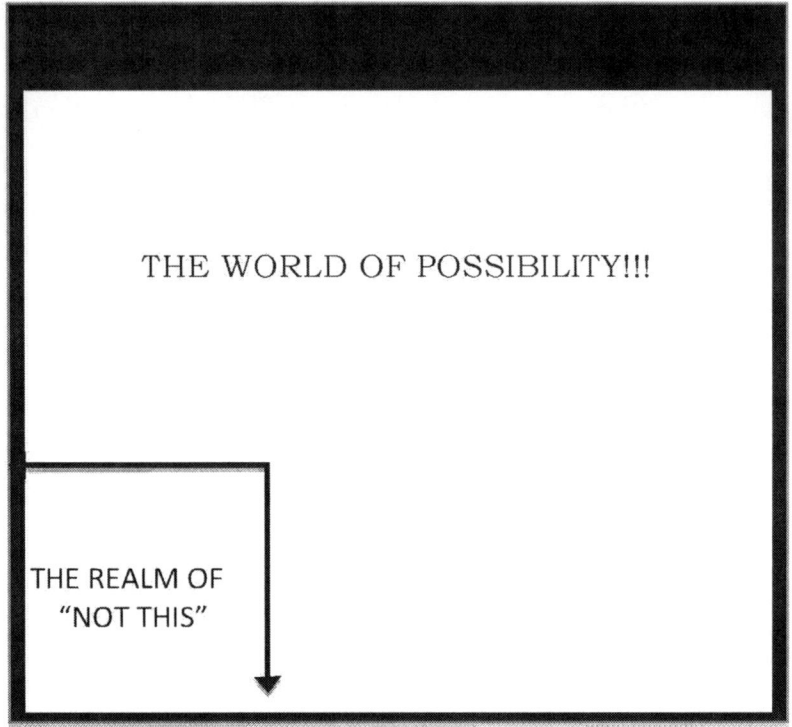

THE WORLD OF POSSIBILITY!!!

THE REALM OF
"NOT THIS"

Being able to move from one place, wherever you are now, to a new place takes a blend of faith and courage. Faith means different things to different people. I won't go into all that it could mean. In this instance, let me simply define it as getting out of your own way. Get out of your head, stop the chatter, and take a step.

If you know where you want to go, that's great! If you know where you don't want to go, then any step away is a step in the right direction. New information comes with each new step you take. That means you can make additional choices with each new step. To make the process a little easier, I've outlined seven stages you'll go through as you recognize you want something different from what you have now:

1. Desire

2. Definition

3. Decision

4. Determination

5. Dedication

6. Discernment

7. Destination

Start with wanting something. It's okay. Want something. Want a specific something. Want to get away from a specific something. For some it's a person, a job, or a situation that seems to keep occurring. If you can define the "not this," then you can get to a place of making a positive statement. Let's say you know you don't want your bank account to be overdrawn again. The "not this" is simply to never overdraw again! The "this" or positive turnaround to the "not this" is to have enough money to be able to get by without having to pay bank fees. The bigger "this" is to become financially independent, a goal way beyond just getting by. From there, you then focus on how to achieve that positive goal by spending less and earning more. Though it seldom feels easy to attain at first, it gets easier and becomes doable when you get clear about your desire.

Allow yourself to *desire*.

Desire is different from the second step of *definition*. You have to be okay with wanting something different. If you made a decision that seemed right at the time and yet you realize you are slowly dying, it's okay to want things to be different. This step is about creating a well-defined focus for what you *want* and actively seeking feedback along the way.

Define that desire. What, exactly, do you want?

» Money in my bank account

» Be specific: A minimum of $1,200 in my checking account with an average balance of $3,800. My savings will be ten times the average balance of my checking, and my portfolio will be at least thirty times my savings. Now that's pretty specific. (Note, you don't have to shoot for those specific numbers; aim higher!)

» A relationship that works

» Think in terms of specifics. Starting with what you don't want is okay, and to get to what you actually do want you have to move beyond it. Don't get stuck in what it isn't. That is, it's *not* "not him." The specifics of "anyone but this person" is a good start, as it certainly could be the other person who has some traits, habits, or issues you choose not to deal with any longer. You just may be at a point of having had enough and need to be by yourself or with someone completely different. That's fine; sometimes that happens. The message here is to get clear about what you *do* want and not to stay focused on the things or people you don't want. If it's "not him," then you need to get clear about who or what you want so you don't jump from one relationship that doesn't work to another and another that could be dysfunctional in the exact same way. If you're honest with yourself, you'll be able to reflect on the part you played in how the relationship got to where it is. It could be that you and your partner find your way to a therapist or relationship coach to help you create the relationship you really want. It could be that you simply have to put the other person in the realm of *not this*. Okay, so define what a "working relationship" means to you, what you'll put into it, and how you'll create what you want by putting yourself in the world differently. To attract the right person, you have to be attractive. This isn't about outward beauty; you need to be someone to whom people could be attracted. As with any of this work on getting better, the question is what energy are you giving to whom and how? Take some time to reflect on how a positive relationship would feel, how you'd know you were in one, and how you might go about creating that. Decide that and you'll have your answers about finding (creating) a good, solid relationship.

» A job that treats me well and rewards me well

» Define what that job looks like, where it is, what kind of work it is, the kind of people you'll be working with, and how much you'll be paid to do it. The clearer you become, the more likely it is that you'll find opportunities that align with who you are. Old resumes used to have an objective statement at the top. Develop your objectives, not for a resume but perhaps for your vision board. Get clear. Write it down. Focus.

You might be noticing that each step leads to the next. Dare to *desire* something. *Define* specifically what it is. Then move to the third step: *decision*. *Decide* that you can actually pursue it.

» I *can* control my finances.

» I *can* have a relationship that works.

» I *can* create a job that is rewarding.

One of the keys to the decision step is that you have to decide that you're worthy of having the things you desire. Here's where Decisions Terminate Panic, though just thinking about it might cause a little panic. You'll be stronger when you write these statements down and speak them aloud.

» I'm worthy of having a stable financial situation.

» I'm worthy of having a relationship that works.

» I'm worthy of having a rewarding job where my contributions are acknowledged and rewarded.

None of the things on your list are done in isolation (unless your defined desire was to become a hermit in a cave on a hillside somewhere). You need to engage with people—to give, to listen, to value, and to receive. Decide that you're worthy of giving to others and receiving rewards as a result.

Once you've decided that you really want something and that you are worthy of receiving it, the next step is *determination*. You really, really have to commit to it. If you can't commit to your decision, you're left floating along in the world of wishes. You'll continue to live at the whim of someone else. That's how you got here. And now you're growing. You're daring to desire. You're getting clearer and defining what you want. You've decided to go for it, and now you're truly committing to your decision. You are engaging in a contract with yourself. "I won't stop till I reach my goal."

That's dedication! Well actually, dedication is all about engaging in the work that it takes to get there. Up until now it's been about your emotional and mental states. Once you've gotten clear about what you want, you're on your way to making it happen. Now you need to dedicate yourself to finding, building, and using the resources you have and get to where you've determined deep down you want to be.

It's so hard to make this kind of commitment. Yeah. It is *easier* to wish and hope and dream; you know that will only take you to the land of wishes, hopes, and dreams. Taking action steps to actually do something will lead to positive change. Dedicating yourself to changing your life for the better, even just a little, means that you've begun Choosing Your Power.

Dedication is about making a strategic plan. *How* will you ensure the continuation of that step-by-step, moment-by-moment process of staying present and truly Choosing Your Power? What will you do? What will you commit to doing? By showing up differently in the world and giving of yourself, you'll be positioning yourself to get what you need. It's sort of symbiotic. You'll feel like you're giving, and you'll be waiting for the payoff. The trick is to show up as worthy and give to those who need your unique talents. It's that action that serves to create a change in you for the better. Ask yourself what you will give to others so that ultimately you can be acknowledged for the worthy self you've said you are.

Reflect on the steps so far: You've dared to *desire*, *defined* what it is you really, really want, *decided* to go for it, and have become *determined* that no one can stop you, not even you. You're *dedicating* yourself to a plan to stay in the moment and really actively engage in Choosing Your Power by *discerning* whether what you're doing is getting you closer to or further from your goal.

Discernment is a critical part of this process. You need to evaluate what you're doing and whether it's working for you. Remember that course correction thing an aircraft does? Well, you've identified your landing strip. So is what you're doing right now getting you closer to or further from your goal?

Is the progress you've made getting you closer to the thing you defined? Course corrections can be made in an instant. If you've decided that you want to shed some pounds you don't need and you end up with a pizza and ice cream in your shopping cart, you have choices. Put them back, or if they're already home, throw them out. Part of dedication is paying for your lessons. Discernment means that you're being honest about the feedback you're getting. Take a good look at the path and action steps you've chosen; are they working for you?

Each of these steps goes hand in hand. You've probably noticed that you can't simply jump from desire to destination. You need to know what you want and what it looks like specifically and commit to getting there. Then you need to take the steps to get there and along the way evaluate whether those steps are working. You could be making progress much more slowly than you'd like. That's different from getting feedback that you're no longer headed in the right direction.

Eventually you'll arrive at your desired *destination*. You wanted this thing. You worked hard for it. Destination doesn't mean stopping. Landing takes work too. Wow, this life thing, it's a conscious process. Be aware, get clear, and then get out of your own way. Once you've gotten the job, partner, house, bank account, or specific weight that you want, you have to work to maintain it. That doesn't mean you don't get to enjoy it. Enjoy working on it. Some people like working on cars to get them purring perfectly. Some people like working in the garden for enjoyment that comes from harvesting the fruits and vegetables or gathering the blossoming flowers. None of that happens by itself. If left untended, a garden becomes a dirt patch filled with weeds. How you show up and what you give determines what you get back. By the way, you can't plant pumpkins and expect cantaloupe. You need to focus on what you want and create the conditions needed to get it. Got it?

This whole process involves becoming clear about what you want and eliminating what you don't want. It may seem odd to have read this many pages about the simple act of deciding to decide. The thing is, people will forgive you for making what may turn out to be a bad decision if you acknowledge the error. Remember that course correction thing? Let's say you get feedback that you are heading down the wrong path. There's nothing wrong with owning the error as long as you also show that you're taking action to correct your course. Imagine what would happen if a pilot let his or her plane get blown off course and didn't pay attention to it or make any course corrections. Yes, things happen. People find out that they're heading down the wrong paths as they journey to where they said they wanted to be. Mistakes are forgivable, but the bigger lesson is that no one forgives *not* making a decision or *not* taking action.

Remember that it's okay to risk making a decision. Not only is it okay, but you have to risk making a decision if you're going to move beyond where you are now. Decisions *do* terminate panic as you take action, pay attention to the feedback you receive, and step-by-step find ways to continue Choosing Your Power!

CHAPTER 6

Envisioned Positive Outcome

THE LAST CHAPTER OFFERED YOU the steps to move from wanting something to actually getting it. The truth is that it's easier to read than to do what it takes to make it happen. So let's back up a bit and develop a stronger foundation for getting there. You have the understanding of the process. That whole thing about decisions terminating panic makes sense. The problem is that it's often quite difficult to make the initial decision about what you *want*. The other problem is that if you don't know specifically where you're going, you won't know if you're on the right track or even when you've arrived.

It's not easy to define the end goal or determine your Envisioned Positive Outcome (or what I call the **EPO**). This chapter will walk you through that a little bit more. Most people begin by knowing what feels bad. They know what they don't want. You may not be able to use words to define what it is you don't want specifically. You may have a feeling. In fact, your language likely reflects your dissatisfaction with your current situation: "I hate running" or "Ugh, I'm so fat" or "My butt is too big" or "Doing this report for work sucks" or "I don't have enough money." The list is endless, and the language—whether you say this to yourself with all of those voices you have in your head (what I call your internal committee) working overtime or say it out loud to a family member, friend, or coworker—only focuses on the negative.

Your subconscious is ready to help you get the very thing on which you focus.

So let's look at the language examples above. Read through them again and see how they might play out in your life if you were the one to say them.

> » *I hate running.* The subconscious takes this information and says, "Great! Let's get an injury or put on so much weight that we won't have to *or* so that we can enjoy hating running. Done deal!"

> » *Ugh, I'm so fat.* Yep! You've made a declaration and "decided" what you want, thereby inviting your subconscious to go to work making that statement an end goal. You end up getting a

yes from your subconscious. And *poof!* You find that you're not burning fat efficiently, your sleep is off, and you're not getting not what you were wishing for. Wishing and taking action are two different things. Even small steps like doing one thing differently at a time can bring the stability to your life you had hoped was possible. Or you could continue on as you have been. *Hmmm ... more chips? Well, they are thin chips, and I can eat a bunch without too many calories ... Now where's that dip?*

» *My butt is too big.* Aren't you lucky that you find ways to sit and not exercise? In addition to finding it harder to get off the couch or out of bed, your food choices will support your statement as well. Certainly, your clothing will give you clear evidence and validate this statement. And this way, other people can vote for your statement of truth too.

» *Doing this report for work sucks.* While it's probably more true that not doing the report for work would suck worse, doing the report may very well just plain suck. Doing it only throws a spotlight on your feeling underappreciated already at work (or dishes at home or preparing taxes or whatever it is that sucks in the moment). The thing is, you have a powerful pilot that agrees to the directions you give. That subconscious mind focused on affirmation picks up your statement and says, "Yeah, let's see how much it *can* suck." So not only will doing the report suck, and you'll find all kinds of reasons or evidence, but the report itself—the end product—might suck as well. Rather than looking at the resources you have available, you'll find all kinds of things that aren't working for you, and you'll end up staying late, struggling to get it all done, and even producing something far inferior to what you're capable of. That will serve to reinforce the statement that the "doing" did in fact suck. The report and the work of doing it really will feel bad to you. Congratulations on that *yes* you got.

» *I don't have enough money.* Sure thing! We can all find things upon which to spend our money. We make choices based on the things we value. Quite often we end up needing to feel good in a particular moment. Therein lies the danger of the impulse buy. Who doesn't love getting parcels in the mail? But then what arrives isn't as useful as you first thought. The money goes, and you confirm, "I don't have enough money." The cycle starts again as the subconscious picks this affirmation up. You will find that there continues to be more month than money. That's rough because you'll focus on where you look. If you're riding a bike and staring at a hole in the road, you'll drive toward that hole. If you're focused on what you *don't* have, you'll continue to only see what's missing from your life and may even compare your condition against what other people have and then create a greater sense of lack (partly because you'll be tempted to buy things to make up for feeling badly). Chemicals released in your brain help in the secret pact your subconscious has in saying "yes," as well. You literally *feel* better buying. Then you feel badly, so you buy more to feel better. Unfortunately, that cycle is based on the things you've been telling yourself and the tools you've had available to help you cope up to this point. As you gain new tools, you will gain a new awareness of your own growth potential.

The concept of FOMO (fear of missing out) is the practice of focusing on what you don't have and hoarding in case you don't get a chance to have something again. Have you ever been to a buffet? A buffet is an opportunity to make appropriate choices. Think of it like a supermarket; just because they sell something doesn't mean it has to end up in your cart. But most people don't think that way at a buffet. Most people don't go and tell themselves they only want to taste a bit of this and/or a bit of that. Most people go and take full helpings (or two or three) because they paid for it, want to get the full value for it, and feel they might miss out on something if they don't try it. Stop it! That kind of thinking will kill you! If you change your thoughts to focus on what you want rather than what you don't have, you'll have greater success in creating the conditions (setting, environment, tools, etc.) for getting there.

In the last chapter, I described how to put the "not this" stuff in a corner. That means that everything else is open for you. It's a possible *yes*. The thing is, you have to keep focusing on the "what's possible" and not what's in the corner.

Your task is to start making different statements and see what kind of action your (quite powerful) subconscious mind sets in motion. Run through the above statements again. I'm not talking about wishful thinking or simple statements of affirmation. Focus on rewriting the script you've given yourself to live. Those tools got you to this place. Congratulations, really. You survived and are now in a different place, ready to make different choices! Review the statements you took (past tense) on as yours. This time focus on the outcome you really want rather than making judgments about how things are (thereby creating a state of "always will be").

The statements modified from above to become more positive look something like this:

» My body craves exercise and responds quickly by producing vibrant and vital health. I've overcome the inertia of just sitting. Now by moving even a little, I can move some more, and my body responds so well! By doing a little more today than I did yesterday, I'm headed in the right direction!

» There are areas of my body that I'm actively sculpting, and I'm deliberately shedding extra weight this efficient body no longer needs.

» I've committed to giving my best to my work. I have the resources I need to produce what's necessary and contribute in such a positive way that my value becomes further recognized. (As you say this and begin to believe it, it's possible that other job opportunities will open up for you. Some that you never even thought of for yourself may appear!)

» My relationship with money is evolving nicely. We're becoming friends, and I recognize that as I contribute to the relationship, I'm rewarded in return. By tracking my accounts and my credit score, I'm able to use positive metrics to make better and better choices to reach my thresholds, milestones, and the finish line.

The last chapter invited you to look at your sense of worthiness and decide what you want and deserve. It laid the groundwork for you to focus on your destination. The essential element is that you *set out toward a particular destination*. This essential element permeates all parts of your life.

It's like a road trip and we need to focus on the specifics:

—Hey, we're headed to the West Coast!

—Okay, but is that Washington, Oregon, or California? (At least we know that we can put "not east" in the corner, and if we head west, we're heading in the right direction.)

—Specifically, we're going to California.

—Okay, but is that Southern California, Central Coast, Bay Area, or Northern California?

—Bay Area!

—Okay, but what part of the Bay Area? Southern? San Francisco? North Bay? East Bay? (We begin to sharpen the envisioned positive outcome as other parts of possibility fall away and become part of the "not this" section of thinking.)

—San Francisco!

—Okay. We're heading west, and we're going to San Francisco. See you there! *Not so fast!* San Francisco is forty-nine square miles. What part of San Francisco are we going to?

—We're going to Pier 39!

—Okay. Well, there are lots of places on Pier 39. Are we going to a restaurant, a shop, or an attraction, or are we just hanging over the side, looking at the sea lions?

—We're going to the end of Pier 39. Keep going past the carousel; we'll head to where the street performers entertain crowds at the end of Pier 39.

—*Okay!*

Though that may seem like a lot of detail to go through, you're now much clearer about what you'll be doing and seeing. It's much clearer than just "We're going on a road trip!"

The same clarity is needed for your mindset as you head anywhere you really want to go. "I want to lose weight" or "I need to make more money" or "I need to be in a different relationship" would be like saying, "I'd like to go on a road trip." What weight do you want to be? How much money do you want as a minimum balance in your checking account? What kind of partner do you want in your life? Once you have clarity, you know where you're headed. It means you're clear and can now make choices about whether or not to stop off for side trips along the way. Stopping at the carousel on the way to the stage at the end of the pier might be worthwhile. You can choose once you have your end point, or—as the title of this chapter says—your envisioned positive outcome (EPO) in mind.

Knowing what you want is exactly like being clear about where you're headed on your own road trip. Once you know what you want, you are able to use a new tool you didn't even know you picked up: discernment. If where you're heading doesn't match your EPO, then it's not part of the road trip this time.

That sounds so easy. And in theory it is. Your job is to practice, to *consciously* put your mind on the things you want to see more of in your life. Want more humor? Find ways to bring it to other people. Want harmony? Find ways to create it without giving your *self* away in the process.

Sometimes there are obstacles in the way of what seems like easy success. The car needs fuel or breaks down on the road trip. It's important to recognize that this road isn't easy to travel, especially if it's new for you. If it's new for you, it will be new for others in your life too. Those others may have a vested interest in you *not* changing, evolving, learning, and growing. Last chapter you decided with determination and dedication that you wanted to do something different, to be different. Now you need to keep that EPO in mind.

You may feel like the only way to get what you want is to make sure that everyone else has what *they* want or need first. You're used to doing that. As the one to keep the peace and "make nice," you were (again past tense) good at giving to others while giving your *self* away. Now, as someone who dares to look at what you want as you value yourself, you'll have to be aware of potential obstacles and other diversions:

> » *People who count on you being the same as you've always been*—there are people in your life who need you to continue to be who you were. You know that you can either grow or wither and shrink. As you learn new things and

begin to use your newfound knowledge, you'll find that others will resist your changing role. At work, at home, or in your other social circles, as you become more powerfully engaged in the world, people will feel uncomfortable around you. Notice it and ride it out. You don't have to fix it. You don't have to "play dumb." You don't have to listen to the judgment of others.

» *Fear of judgment*—some people freeze because of the fear of judgment. The truth is that judgment will be there whether you move forward or not. People may say things to test you. Some may say things because they couldn't dare walk the (new) path you've chosen. Judgment exists, and what others think about you isn't of any concern to you! You're allowed to have ideas, opinions, and value. You're allowed to all of a sudden know what you want and set the conditions to get to your own EPO!

» *Diversions of interest*—what if you're heading down the road and you see something that's really interesting? You have to decide if it's worth stopping for. That carousel on Pier 39 may or may not be something you want to stop for on your way to the stage at the back. You have to decide if it enhances your trip. Those buffet stations offering Chinese food, pizza, and ribs may or may not be of interest to you or worth stopping for on your way to the leaner meats and vegetables. Use your newfound skill of discernment and rule potential diversions in or out along the way. The question to ask is this: *Is what I'm doing right now getting me closer to or further from my goal?* With your EPO in mind, you'll simply know the answer as discernment shows up. (Well done!)

» *Over obligating*—saying yes means you'll need to follow through. Sometimes people who find a new freedom end up overextending themselves by trying too many things all at once. Be careful and pace yourself. If you're already there, step back, look at the big picture, and prioritize. What needs to happen first? Use discernment as you determine whether what you're doing right now getting you closer to or further from your goal? Remember to plan quiet time for yourself because ultimately you can't keep going if you're running on fumes. You've got to refuel. Saying yes at the expense of yourself is just repeating an old habit. You know too much now to let that happen.

So how do you get it done? How do you get any of it done while continuing to head in the right direction without feeling like you're being condemned at every step? Do you remember chapter 3, titled "Permission Granted"? Roger Bannister didn't wait for anyone's permission to cut ahead of the pack in the 1950s and break the four-minute-mile record. If you've truly envisioned *your* positive outcome, then you cannot let anyone or anything interrupt that.

Once you get started, you will be blown off course. It's inevitable. Your focus must then be on how to most efficiently and effectively return to a course or select a new course to bring you to *your* Envisioned Positive Outcome.

Will you get resistance? Yes! A plane gets resistance from facing into the wind. But that's the only way it gets the lift it needs to create flight! You'll get resistance. Use it as a trigger to lift you higher and make you better! You'll be challenged to think of new ways to get better. That's not a bad thing! Welcome challenges as opportunities to ask better questions. Sometimes people give up when they feel any resistance at all. You'll come to a point of embracing the feeling, actually needing to feel it, and then using it to build upon. That's a hard concept right now when it's scary to even face into the wind. People will tell you that you can't follow your path, that it isn't safe, or that it will upset them or someone else. What they're telling you is that they wouldn't do it. The truth is that they couldn't do what you're doing, and they're envious. Take flight and then choose the direction that brings you to your EPO.

You can watch yourself go through this process:

Resistance → Imagination (EPO) → Harmony
→ Realization → Actualization

Resistance demands imagination to become truly clear about your EPO and thereby overcome the resistance.

Imagination demands certain discernment so you can decide upon the best route to take to actually reach your EPO. Once your route is set, don't force the process; *live* the process. Only by living in harmony with the process will other doors open that allow you to realize your EPO smoothly and efficiently. Is it work? Yes. Does it have to be a struggle? No.

This isn't the easiest concept to grasp. We each engage in the worthy struggle of overcoming daily obstacles. We know there's more to life, and we hope, wish, and even pray for a better life. It's not until we become clear about what *better* means that we begin to create it. When we can see the potential to be different, we put energy into being different. Look back at the significant changes you've made at any point in your life. What were you thinking or feeling? What inner dialogue did you have? You somehow knew that things were going to change. That "knowing" was your focus at work—even subconsciously—to get you to a different place. There are steps you'll need to take every day to get to your new place. If you were to learn a new language, you'd practice every day. You couldn't force the process of learning; you could simply practice more until you became proficient. By doing so, you essentially would be creating a new you.

It's the hardest work you'll ever love as you watch yourself develop in spite of—and because of—the comments and "support" you receive from others. It is your current state of discomfort that is prompting you to become different.

Actualization is the transformative place. You haven't just reached your end result, your very own Envisioned Positive Outcome, you've *become* it. You haven't just learned French, for example; you've become a French speaker. Artistic endeavors are the easiest to track along this progression. Resistance comes from outside critics as well as from the treacherous internal critic. After deciding that you truly wish to interrupt the criticism and do something different, you determine what that different thing is. You discern "not this" from "this," and you create a path. Following the steps in that path creates clarity and a certain harmony that others gravitate toward. While some doors open, more resistance comes, and you face a critical choice: you can regress to the comfortable way things were and don't make waves or you can fortify your resolve to stay on your path.

You'll get there. When you reach your desired outcome, you will find yourself driven to start the process again. Artists *must* create. Developers *must* develop. Authors *must* write! So after you've produced your first new "thing," whether it's a bank account total, a particular weight, or an actual product, you'll determine whether that was a finish line or whether getting there caused a transformation. You'll check in with yourself, take regular inventory, and determine if you're becoming the person driven to express yourself and continue to learn and grow as you continue Choosing Your Power.

I have friends who have yo-yoed with their weight on various diets. I also have a friend, Lisa, in Australia who began a difficult path. She knew what she didn't want.

What she wanted seemed really far away. She made a decision and imagined and envisioned her positive outcome. Only by keeping that in mind did she overcome the resistance she encountered along the way. In so doing, she also opened many new doors for herself. She burned through a couple *hundred* pounds and transformed her body. She could have stopped as she approached the weight she once thought was so out of reach. Instead, she became a trainer, teacher, and inspiration to others who didn't think they had a chance. She didn't just realize her goal; she transformed her life to become a new person.

And so can you.

Here are the basic rules: Remember energy gets energy. When you take the first step, you're moving! That's a positive no matter which direction you go, since you can always course correct. In the process, focus on the positive. Being "up" puts other people in the path of your positive vibe. That means you need to put any negative thoughts in the past tense. Think about the end result, the outcome you really want—even if it seems ridiculously difficult to achieve (your bank account, your weight, the people you attract in your life, the project you want to get done, etc.). Don't look for anyone else's permission. Remember, permission granted. Keep your EPO in mind, and do the hard work without forcing the process. Look for new doors to open to allow you opportunities along the way that will help you reach your goal. They're there. You have to accept them and discern which are opportunities and which are distractions.

When you reach your goal, don't stop. Instead reflect. Are you done, or are you just beginning? When martial artists reach the black belt level, they understand that they have been transformed as people and truly are just at a place to understand anew and truly begin learning. For some, the black belt *is* the goal and the end point. A lot of martial artists quit martial arts after being granted the black belt. For others, it's just the beginning. You decide.

You're on a journey, and you will fight real and imagined obstacles. You'll fight ego—yours and other people's. People will want to be better than you. You'll wonder if you're good enough. You'll be afraid. Fear is a huge obstacle in your journey. There are a lot of leaps of faith that you'll force yourself to take. When you realize you don't need to know it all or have the entire plan laid out for every single thing you do, your life becomes a whole lot easier and you, as a person, exude a whole new life-filled energy and become fun to be around.

You might be fighting obstacles related to time. Later in this book, we'll explore concepts of feeling overwhelmed and how to handle constraints of time. It's a real—and manageable—issue. Don't let it be anything other than a hurdle over which you'll leap gracefully. People complain that they don't have enough money. Again, it's a reasonable complaint. Don't let it be a stopper. You can work with the tools you have. You can do *something* with each of the resources you have. Decide where you're headed and whether any of the assets you're utilizing—time, energy, money—are getting you closer to where you really truly want to be.

In addition to the obstacles discussed above, distance has been noted as a factor that causes people not to achieve what they really want. If your goal is to climb Mount Everest, you *are* going to need to get closer to the mountain. If your goal is to be a better photographer, be a decent gardener, learn to speak French, or have a better relationship, you'd do well to start in your own home or backyard. Don't count on others to fix it for you. Start with you and become clear on your destination. This chapter is about envisioning something positive for yourself. What do you have in mind? Don't focus on a road full of obstacles; keep your focus on the horizon ... your destination.

You have to start though. So choose. What is it you want? What is *your* EPO? Take a moment to reflect and write it down. Write your desired outcomes in all the categories you'd like. Make a list. By writing it out, the outcomes become more real and less like unattainable goals or empty wishes. Refer back to what you've written. Then reflect on what you have been through and where you're heading.

Focus on where you want to be. Bring it into your mind's eye, and before you know it you will be enjoying the goal that was at one time so far away. It starts with pushing through resistance and then recognizing something better is available. Choose. Enjoy the power of choice and *your* EPO, the Envisioned Positive Outcome on your path of Choosing Your Power!

Chapter 7

Communication Magic for Your Daily Life

Y OU'VE HEARD THE EXPRESSION, "WATCH your mouth!" It's usually issued as a parental warning to a teenager about foul language, but the advice actually offers guidance for each of us.

The language we use matters. It molds our mind-sets and our relationships at home, at work, and in the community. Our language affects our self-esteem and our presentation in the world, second by second and day-by-day. So you now have a list. Watch your life as you watch your mouth! Your world will open up, and your relationships will become stronger. You will build greater rapport with others using language that connects your ears to their hearts and back again. All of these things are possible as you choose—and use—your vocabulary wisely.

You might not have even known that you were putting an obstacle in the way of communication. You might have been genuinely curious when you asked "why?". And you might have even been trying to be exceptionally helpful when you offered, "You know what you should do?" Unfortunately, those questions didn't serve to get you closer to the other person. If you were observant, you might have watched the person withdraw from you as you initiated an interrogation and then poked him or her with the "right" answer.

My list of ten watchwords encourages you to watch your language. While these words need not be eliminated from your vocabulary altogether, you will enhance your relationships and rapport with others as you choose alternatives. When you "watch" what you're saying, you'll find yourself in a state of simple curiosity, asking different questions to actually get the answers—and successes—you desire and deserve.

So stay curious and discover the outcomes and engagement that you might hope for as you use alternative words to those on the following list.

WAYNE'S TOP TEN WATCH WORDS TO CREATE COMMUNICATION MAGIC IN YOUR DAILY LIFE!

» Why

» But

» Should

» Try

» Maybe

» Can't

» Need

» Always

» Never

» You (as a sentence starter)

Other words of which to be mindful include the possessive preposition of illness. Read on for explanations of each word.

WHY

Unless you're a scientist and *need* to deconstruct a current position, eliminating the word *why* from your vocabulary allows you to ask questions that really get to the answers you want. Usually when I make that claim, someone asks me why.

Think about the answer you get when you ask (or are asked) why questions. The first word of the answer has to be *because*. That's a defensive response, and it doesn't lead to the real answer you're after, unless you're a bully or trying to pick a fight. The response *because* stems from two places. The first is that of submission and defensiveness; someone will need to get the "right" answer to a question beginning with *why*, or else they are wrong or otherwise perceived as bad or less than.

The opposite of being submissive with a because response is a response accompanied with bravado and a louder push back on the person asking the initial question: "Because I wanted to, that's why!"

So a why question elicits a childlike response of defensive hiding from being bad or wrong, or it elicits an obstreperous adolescent argumentative tone.

Either way, if you're interrogating someone with a why question, you're not getting the answer you truly desire unless you're a bully and want someone to cower and give up or you want to pick a fight just for the sake of it. If that's the case, you might want to be more honest with yourself and others with whom you're in a relationship and simply say what you mean from the outset.

The good news is that's not who you are. You're reading this book because your intentions are good. So my belief about you is that you didn't mean to push the other person away.

If you eliminate the word *why*, what's left? That's right! *What* is left! Stay curious and practice using *what* or *how* to get to the true answers you're after.

Think about the answers you'd get (or give) for each of the following why questions and their what or how alternatives:

» Why are you wearing that today?

» What about that appealed to you?

» Why are you late again?

» How can we create a schedule to keep you on time?

» Why are you so upset?

» What are you're feeling so upset about?

When a person doesn't have to justify his or her being, he or she can focus more on creating conditions for being better. You can help others become better by asking better questions! No more *why*. From now on, use *what* or *how* to get to the real answer while helping the other person get there too. You can even ask others to rephrase their questions to you when you are facing the question of why. Better still, rephrase their questions for them:

» Why are you late?

» You mean what happened that traffic was so bad? Boy, I don't know!

Engaging in that way takes the focus away from the personal attack, provides an answer, and subtly trains the other person that *why* doesn't get you to cower anymore. You have new tools!

BUT

Really, there's no room for a *but* unless you are set on undoing something said. Attorneys may have this in their arsenals. Listen for it and understand that *but* only undoes anything that comes before it. It also makes the person using it seem a little snooty or "better than."

» You have on white running shoes, *but* I have on black slip-ons.

» Subtext: my shoes are better than yours.

» Our numbers were really good the past couple of months, *but* we have two weeks left in this one!

» Subtext: You're all doing terribly this month! What's wrong with you?

This was a real example of a manager attempting to motivate his team. He didn't realize that one little word could undo his good intentions! If you take those same sentences and substitute the word *and* for the word *but,* you can make the meaning of the sentence one that is inclusive and uplifting:

» You have on white running shoes, *and* I have on black slip-ons.

» Subtext: we're both wearing cool shoes (i.e. we're both okay!).

» Our numbers were really good the past couple of months, *and* we have two weeks left in this one!

> » Subtext: We can do as well this month as we have done the last couple of months! Let's make it happen!

Once I saw a main character on a TV show accuse one of the other leads of making a "but face": the face you make just before saying the word *but*. Be aware of that yourself. All too often we're thinking of a rebuttal to something before the other person has finished talking. *Yeah but* ... comes out all across our faces. The remedy is to think in terms of *yes and*. By staying inclusive, you listen to what the other person has to say, and then you build upon it, not tear it down to make yourself more right than he or she is. (This is another topic we will address in a different chapter. For now, focus on your language!) Additionally, stop yourself from creating an answer before the other person has finished speaking. When you're busy rebutting in your head, you miss what the other person is saying.

Your new life-changing tool is here: substitute the word *and* anytime you find yourself wanting to say *but*. You'll see how people feel more included and less defensive around you. Wow, that one little word makes a huge difference!

SHOULD

Another favorite word for elimination is the power-word of the committee that lives in your head: you really *should* ... Accompanying such language comes an implied (or occasionally outwardly expressed) wag of the finger, letting you know how bad, wrong, or lazy you are. If you use the word *should* against yourself, you're continuing to devalue yourself and your efforts to do better in the world. If you wield that word against someone else, you're aggressively pushing that person away, as he or she only feels your judgment. Bullies use such language to belittle others or to imply their judgment of them as wrong or bad. Such language is toxic.

I laughed when I first heard that , "Shoulds are shit," and what I learned is that people really needn't *"should"* all over themselves or anyone else for that matter. I hope that makes sense to you because the outcome of using or hearing "should" is that someone feels badly.

Think about the implied meaning of each sentence when the *should* word comes up:

» You know what you *should* do is ...

It often comes up when someone not in your situation gives you advice about how to run your life, though he or she would never do what he or she is suggesting to you. That's a heavy should to take on.

Other forms of should come in the past tense and sound like scolding for something not done:

» I really *should* have taken a different route; there's so much traffic on this one.

» You *shouldn't* have eaten that.

» You *should* have been here sooner.

These are impossible to remedy. The thing is done. You can't change it without a time machine. So what is available now?

>   Did you set out on your journey to get stuck in traffic on purpose? No. So judging yourself as bad or wrong doesn't serve you.

>   Knowing that you've overeaten doesn't get better when you judge yourself as bad or wrong. Seek positive choices in that moment.

>   Once you've arrived, you can't be there any sooner. That is, being scolded for not being somewhere sooner doesn't help. Do you need to demonstrate that you're bad and wrong and miserable for not being there sooner, or can you do something now to make the most of being there?

Exchange the words *would* or *could* for the word *should*. What is in your power to do now? What would or could you do currently or in the near future to make the most of what you have? More powerfully, what choices can you make about what you *want* to do, especially as you move toward your Envisioned Positive Outcome!

Ask different questions and get better answers. Punish yourself and stay stuck, or use different words—those of possibility—and truly stay present in the process of Choosing Your Power!

TRY

Our ancient, wise friend Yoda says, "Do or do not. There is no try." Such sage advice you would expect from a Jedi master. Look at the words and let them ring for you. People don't really try; they either do something or they don't do it. According to popular mythology, Fritz Perls, the founder of Gestalt psychology was noted to have to have said in various seminars and workshops, "Trying is lying." Both Yoda and Perls indicate that you aren't being truthful with yourself or with others when you say that you'll try. It's about committing.

What message are you really hearing when someone tells you, "Yeah ... I'll *try* to pick you up at 7:30." Can you count on that person being there? In this case, *try* really does feel like a lie! Wouldn't it be better to hear, "It'll be difficult to get there by 7:30; can I pick you up closer to 7:45?" There's an honesty and promise in that—something that was absent in the statement of try.

» Can you pick your clothes up off the floor?

» I'll try.

» Would you be able to finish that report for me by 2:00?

» Uh, sure, I'll try.

If you don't believe you can accomplish the requested task, say, "No, I won't be able to do that right now." It's so much cleaner than "trying" and then coming up empty or late or wrong.

In some instances, it makes sense to substitute the word *practice* for *try*:

» I can try cooking this dish.

» I can practice cooking till it comes out better.

» I can try to learn Spanish.

» I can practice Spanish and continue to improve.

These first three words on this list—*why*, *but*, and *try*—are essential to eliminate. By purging them from your vocabulary, your life will change. Possibilities will exist where doors were once shut. The rest of the words on the list are important to quarantine and bring out only sparingly.

MAYBE

How many ways can a person lie while being polite? Really. We learned to lie to save a relationship rather than tell the truth. "Ready to buy that car soon?" "Sure, maybe." It's a game of collusion. We've learned to tell people what they want to hear, and on the receiving end, we readily accept a maybe answer as a strong possibility.

A while ago, I briefly considered what it would take to remodel my bathroom. A salesperson called me, and I realized that I really didn't want his company's solution. Instead of saying no outright, I said I wasn't ready to make a decision. I indicated that I needed to think about it more and said, "Sure, *maybe* someone can give me a call back another time." I didn't want to hurt the salesperson's feelings.

It was horrible when I finally realized that I had kept hopeful salesperson after hopeful salesperson on the hook for almost a year. A year! I would get a call. I'd do a polite song and dance and ask to have someone check back with me. As good salespeople, they put my name in a tickler file and handed off my name and number, and someone dutifully called me back. When I came to terms with my folly, I finally simply asked to be taken off of their lists. You know, they almost sounded as relieved as I was. No one really enjoys being strung along to an eventual no, and it took an energetic toll on me to have the next call hanging over me.

You can see how *try* and *maybe* are ways of maintaining a noncommittal state. If you hear them from yourself or from someone else, seek to commit even if it means you won't be popular in that moment. Set real and realistic boundaries and expectations. Your integrity grows and— having already eliminated the apology—you begin to realize that you're entitled to make a statement and not waffle in the wishy-washy land of *maybe* so as not to offend.

CAN'T

When you tell yourself you can't do something, you're exercising language that keeps a past condition current. Just because you haven't done something yet doesn't mean you can't.

In my journey, I struggled with telling myself that I couldn't seem to learn Spanish. The truth is that I hadn't learned Spanish *yet*. I hadn't ever truly studied in earnest or followed through on using those CD courses I bought. Just because I hadn't done something didn't mean I couldn't.

Where have you gotten stuck? Change your language and put behind you the thing that has kept you stuck:

» I can't find the right job.

» I can't find the right person.

» I can't hold onto money.

Don't let it be a present-tense condition. Read the above sentences again. Then read these sentences of opportunity and movement:

» I haven't found a job that seems right for me *yet*.

» In the past, I may not have been open to having the right person show up.

» I used to have trouble holding onto money.

Each of these sentences implies that conditions have changed. They have! You're thinking differently, and in doing so, you're opening yourself to new possibilities!

NEED

Do you truly need anything or anyone? Sure, okay, there are basic needs of food, clothing, and shelter that we must have to survive. When someone puts him or herself at the mercy of someone else, they cease to exist as individuals.

> » I just really need a good man/woman/job/etc.

> » Argh ... I need to win the lottery.

> » I need a large diet cola and a jumbo fries (danger, danger!).

The obvious substitution is *want*. What you want is different than what you need. You give your *self* away when you live in the world of need. There's a desperation that artificially holds you hostage.

Think about what it would mean to you to declare, "I really want_____."

In chapter 5, we traveled from desire to destination. You have to *dare to declare* and not live in the space of mattering so little to yourself or the world.

Declaring your wants allows you to be a person who is deserving.

> » I want and deserve a good person in my life.

» I want and deserve a good job.

» Heck, I want and deserve to win the lottery!

Always/Never

Always and *never* go hand in hand. They're extremes and hardly ever accurate. Couples run into trouble when they accuse each other of *always* being a certain way or *never* doing a certain thing:

» You are *always* late.

» You *never* help around the house.

» I *always* mess up like this.

» I *never* do well in these situations.

Don't those sentences just scream, "Argument coming!" It's true even when you're talking to yourself. Taking responsibility for your feelings and choosing to do something differently brings you to a place of progress.

What would happen if instead of accusing, you claimed your feelings and requested something different for the future?

» I get frustrated when you're late. Can you arrive early the next few times?

» When I'm doing housework and I don't see you participating, I feel put upon. Would you contribute by taking care of the dishes this week?

» Sometimes things don't go the way I'd like. I haven't felt good in those situations, so I'll explore what options are available to me now.

» I've had difficulty (in the past) in these situations. I can approach this one differently by preparing and practicing for various outcomes.

While you seek alternative solutions of various positive possibilities, the substitute word for the always-never trap is *sometimes*.

You (As a Sentence Starter)

Often accompanying the always-never trap, the fight starts with an accusation. The problem is that all too often people use this language against themselves. Whether you say these things to yourself or you hear them from someone else, you've begun an aggressive, demeaning conversation.

» You are so lazy.

» You have a fat butt.

» You suck.

So what language might you now choose? (See what's happening? You can become aware of alternatives and begin to choose to be different! How empowering! How magical!) Use any of the alternatives from above. Begin with *I* and make a feeling statement about your current condition. Put the negative in past tense so that it doesn't stay a current state. What was, *was*!

>> While I feel badly about not having exercised, I can choose to exercise or not. Either way, *I'm* making a choice.

>> Certain parts of my body are pretty darn good. Okay, I want (not need) to work on other parts. What can I do differently to get a different result?

>> I have so many redeeming qualities that there's no room for a broad sweeping negative judgment. In fact, I (declare that I) only want people around me who have supportive, positive language (and that includes me).

By choosing to bring the positive to the current state and put the negative behind you, you've changed your life. The choice *is* the change.

POSSESSIVE PREPOSITION OF ILLNESS

In addition to eliminating these top ten words from your vocabulary, pay attention to the language of illness. Stop using the possessive preposition *my* when talking about a condition:

>> My headache just won't quit.

» I have to go in for another treatment for my cancer.

» My cough that came with my cold just won't quit.

Instead, use a detached neutral word like *the* and call the condition by its symptoms:

» I experienced some throbbing in my head.

» The symptoms of the cancer have begun to abate. My body accepts and makes full use of medication, nutrients, and a program to restore balance and health.

» My body is getting stronger as it has been dealing with the symptoms associated with an upper respiratory condition.

As new personal scripts replace old self-talk, you can feel changes taking place. I know cancer survivors who never "owned" it but rather kept the condition as a neutral diagnosis not belonging to them. Anyone battling with a devastating diagnosis deserves as much leverage as they can get. Given that cancer is so prevalent in our society, it's likely you know someone dealing with the effects of it. Encourage the distance of the symptoms while accepting healthy thoughts and a body that works efficiently to battle that which doesn't belong to it.

One major difference between those who are effective in the world and those who are victims of the world is *locus of control.* Do you believe that you impact the outcome of events in your life? Studies of optimism point to those who believe they are responsible for the good that happens to them. They make choices and think about options for overcoming obstacles, which they see as reasonable challenges. Meanwhile, pessimists believe that anything good that happens to them is probably a fluke and will certainly be followed by something negative. They view the negative as inevitable, not as a challenge for which they have resources.

Thinking about the specific words you use—especially in your self-talk—helps you keep a whole-health focus. What words did we use that unwittingly kept us stuck? Along with eliminating particular words and paying attention to *not* possessing the toxic, another quick example will get you thinking about language choices every day. What does it mean to lose something? Most people have this meme in mind whether they mean to or not: If you lose your cell phone, what do you do? You frantically search to find it! If you lose your keys, you look everywhere to find them. Losing something means that you instinctively and automatically begin the search to find it. And so it goes with weight loss as well.

Aren't you happy that you lost five pounds? Won't you be surprised and disappointed when you find those pounds again? We lose things; we find them. It's time we noticed the language we use to describe attaining our desired weight. Animals shed their winter coats. If you shed five unnecessary pounds, then it really is not necessary to find them.

Listen to the language you use in everyday interactions with others. Listen to the language you use with yourself. Stay focused on your desired outcome and shed the language that's not working.

Oh, and one more note: It's not what you say; it's ... (c'mon, you know what's next). It's not what you say; it's how you say it. Pay attention to the speed or pace of your speech, the pitch that rises under stress or drops to indicate severity or comfort, the tone as it becomes sharp or soothing, and the volume, which can indicate the passion in your message. According to research initiated by Dr. Albert Mehrabian several decades ago, those elements now known as metacommunication accounts for around 38 percent of the meaning received in any message. About 55 percent of the message's meaning comes in the form of facial expression and body language. That's right. Only about 7 percent of the meaning of any message is in the actual words we use. [1]

The way you say "thank you" would change in each of the following situations:

- » Someone tells you that you are a lucky winner in a drawing.

- » A police officer gives you a ticket.

- » You find out someone hit your car.

---

[1]   Mehrabian, A., *Silent Messages: Implicit Communication of Emotions and Attitudes*, Belmont CA: Wadsworth (1981) (currently distributed by Albert Mehrabian, am@kaaj.com)

» You have just learned that what you thought was a serious illness can be easily treated.

The words *thank you* in each instance are identical, but the meaning changes with their delivery. So remember that up to 93 percent of the meaning of your message is in the delivery. That's significant as you engage with others and continue to have conversations with yourself.

By reframing your approach to the world and changing your language (both internal and external), you create room for the better things to be seen, acknowledged, and appreciated. Ultimately, you create a more positive life for yourself as you attract the things you think about. Eliminate the words on the watch-word list that you no longer wish to employ. Begin using the alternate words, the language of health and personal power. The language you use really can be magical and enable you to uncover your emerging strengths. Seek opportunities and possibilities. Hold the negative in the past tense and neutral. Own the positive as you pursue options to grow further, and observe the responses you get as you grow stronger and become someone who is truly quite powerful in the world. As you take these steps, you'll recognize that you really are Choosing Your Power!

CHAPTER 8

Gratitude and Attitude

ON A FLIGHT FROM DALLAS/FORT Worth to San Francisco, I had the pleasure of meeting Jessica, a flight attendant who reminded me about the gift of life and the gratitude we can each bring to every day. With a genuine smile on her face, she politely and cheerfully offered refreshments to the passengers in her section. As my style is to engage, reward came when a simple comment I made about her good cheer at the end of what I knew was a long day led to a conversation wherein she shared her philosophy. She said that her perspective on life's gift had come into focus when a recent freak boating accident had taken from her three people she had known and even raced with.

It could have been anyone. Losing people or things close to us gives us the opportunity to reflect on our own situations. We can become bitter, or we can take stock of what we have and become grateful for our daily gifts, no matter how small. Jessica told me that she *chose* to be cheerful and grateful because she didn't like the alternative.

How amazing it is to be able to look at what you have every day and marvel at the wonder of its being there! When you start each day from a place of true gratitude for the gifts in your life, no matter what those gifts are, your perspective changes.

It's easy to look at the problems. It's easy to look at how much you don't have. Living in lack means that you'll only be dissatisfied with whatever comes your way because it's never going to feel like enough. You won't ever find the right person, the right job, enough money, or the right things to make you feel better. If you've been feeling as if you don't have enough of the right things or as if what you have isn't enough, you're stuck. You may know people like this. You know how much they suck the energy out of everything they—or you—do. If it's you living and approaching the world in this way, you'll question the value of everything from your furniture and your food to your clothes and your car. You'll take them in, and then you'll discount what you've gotten as not good enough anyway.

By this point, you may be experiencing some of the lessons from previous chapters. That's perfect. You'll be able to reflect on how insidious certain styles of thinking can become. The battle to keep positive is one that can only be won by keeping positive. Here, energy gets energy. Focusing on doing something positive builds more positivity.

And when it goes badly, it goes very badly. Such attitudes show up strangely. For example, if you've found yourself overeating or hoarding or buying things because they make you feel good, you may have gotten stuck in a very strange paradox. "It's not enough, so I'll have more of the same." To break free, you must change your perspective and your actions. Take a real inventory. There are people with more things, less debt, and prettier skin. So what? Really. What is that to you? What do you have?

What do you have, not relative to anyone else? What do you have for which you can be grateful? It doesn't matter toward whom you feel gratitude. This isn't about religion, though it may be about "Spirit," whatever that means to you. It's about looking at what you've brought into your life, recognizing that you created everything you have, and appreciating that you can choose what you do with it.

Do you care about the people in your life? If you care, you can be grateful that they're there. Now what actions do you take to show them that you care? What do you do to demonstrate gratitude for what you have? Start small. Stand up and look down. Do you have toes? Are you happy you have toes? If you don't have toes, what's the first thing you see? Oh, and if you're overweight enough that you can't see your toes when you look down, can you be grateful that you've had the good fortune to have been fed?

When you start thinking in those terms, you open the door for greater gifts. You stop looking at what you don't have, and you start finding ways to create more of what you actually want in your life.

Change your language to let go of what hasn't worked in the past. Dare to show up. Yes, again, permission granted. Dare to dream. Yes, again, imagine ... and envision a state you really want to attain. Develop your Envisioned Positive Outcome (EPO). Write down what you want. Be grateful for small steps. Reflect on where you've been, and don't dwell on what might happen. Dwelling on what might happen causes anxiety. Living in *what was* causes depression. Focus on what you want, and plan on how to best get there. What resources do you have? What strategic steps do you need to take?

Did you get that? Ask yourself two key questions:

» What resources do you have?

» What strategic steps do you need to take to use them effectively?

So many people don't even step back to ask themselves those two questions. They stay stuck because it's easier to stay stuck. They worry, whine, moan, and put themselves deeper into the positions they worry, whine, and moan about. Oh, don't get me wrong here; those are terrible places to get stuck. The saying is, "If you're going through hell, keep going." So to get out of a place that isn't working for you, look at what you *do* have.

Start there, with gratitude. Be grateful for what you enjoy. Even the challenges that force you to ask better questions can be held in esteem. It's been said that your attitude determines your altitude. How high you fly is up to you. But is that attitude stuff just a platitude?

Your attitude comes out in everything you do. It isn't done to you; it's something you create from within. Then others react or respond to it ... to you. Attitude is a conscious choice, or at least it can be. What if you chose to see everything that happened in your world as a gift? Yes, bad stuff happens. Tragedy strikes. What if you chose to view difficulties as challenges to overcome? What are you left with?

Here's a fairly innocuous example. It's not tragic; in fact, it's far from it. And though to some people it might seem tragic, I think it serves to illustrate how one incident can color our view of all like situations if we're not aware. Let's say you've been out at a diner, and you paid for your meal with cash. You've already left a tip, and then as you're leaving you realize that the change you received was short. Some people would choose to see that as a direct omen of bad news—that they were chosen to be picked on. From there, they would judge all waitresses as untrustworthy and all clerks as thieves. You've been around people who think like this. They had one bad experience, and they've painted the world as a bad place, especially "those kinds of people," referring to the untrustworthy waitress, or lawyer, or ethnic cohort.

Because of that bad experience, they approach certain type of people with caution. They tip badly and then later have poor service when they show up again because they treated the wait-staff badly. The person that caused the initial domino to fall might not have even known what happened and might not even be there anymore, but still everyone else is being punished for that initial transgression.

Or you make a choice. You return at the point of having been shortchanged and sort it out, noting that it was probably an oversight on the other person's part. Or you make a different choice. You note that the amount you were shorted is not significant enough to warrant your being upset, and you chalk it up as being extra tip. You treat other wait-staff as if they're human and worth interacting with, not as thieves or automatons, and you receive exceptional service. By letting go of a transgression and not taking it personally, you stop carrying it with you.

Men and women vary here. And yes, while this is a sweeping generalization and not true for *everyone*, guys tend to want to fight when their ego becomes bruised. If they've been made to look bad or feel bad, they'll find a way to get payback. That is—and I'm going to an extreme stereotype here—if guys feel as though they've been "wronged," they'll go out of their way to right the wrong by "wronging" someone else. Essentially, they've paid the wrong forward. It's faulty thinking, and it only serves to perpetuate a bad situation. Attitude check time! What if they asked themselves, "What am I missing about this person or situation that might be blocked because I'm choosing to react in this way?" Notice that the power is back in their hands as they take the action of inquiry, insight, and choice of reaction.

Women are great grudge holders, as well as the holders of history. It's seldom about something as trivial as getting the wrong change back. Nope, it's more about the thing you said or didn't say or the way you smiled or didn't smile or the time you were late or ... No, I don't have an ax to grind here, and yes, I'm going to the extreme stereotype again. What's funny is that you're probably holding this book and shaking your head with a smirk on your face because you recognize the behavior as yours or the behavior of someone close to you. So time to check that attitude! What if instead of carrying that trivial incident forward and treating it as if it were the most egregious thing to happen to a person, you choose to create different working agreements in that particular relationship, whether at home or with a store clerk? For example, "This bothered me, and in the future, I'd like ..."

So it's back to choice again! What if when affronted we each took responsibility to say something in the moment about our preferences? What if we took on an attitude of recognizing that the intention of the other person was probably not personal? Honestly, think about the last time something "bad" happened to you: someone didn't greet you the way you wanted, you didn't get the meal prepared the way you wanted, or someone cut you off on the road. Now think about the person who perpetrated that act. Do you think he or she woke up that morning with the intent of making your life miserable? That he or she awoke with the thought, *Ha-ha ... today I'm going to really get to [insert your name here] and make his/her life miserable. [Insert evil cackle here.]*

Okay, if—and there is a possibility—*if* the person you thought about really had that intent, you need to get some support and get out of that relationship! Seriously. No fooling. Get help.

What's more likely is that the other person either doesn't know you or he or she actually likes you; the person could have his or her own backstory for his or her day playing out. You know that he or she didn't intend to harm you or hurt your feelings. How you respond then becomes a deliberate choice, *your* choice.

I just had a great experience at a restaurant in a really small town in Texas. Austin—the waiter, not the town—was sweating and looking frazzled when a group of eight of us plus a baby came in for lunch. He had obviously had quite a morning. We, as a group, were focused on being the group we were. He approached us with caution and low energy, and he really just seemed like he wanted to be the order taker and get this painful lunch service over with.

When it came time to order, I was elected to go first. He was standing a few feet from the table, angled behind me, which required me to twist awkwardly over my shoulder just to see him. Oh, and I always look at the people I talk to, even waiters. I started by turning fully around and then introduced a question.

Facing him and smiling, I said, "Hey … good afternoon! What's your name?" He told me his name. Still smiling, with an encouraging tone I used his name, saying, "Austin, you look like you've had quite a morning already. Do this for me, okay? Take a breath, relax, and smile. It's all good."

He did just that. He took a breath, dropped his shoulders, and smiled. Austin went on to explain that there had been an unexpected catering party of forty people he had to attend to, and then another group of twenty had shown up unexpectedly. He was assigned to both. Then our large group had come in. As he spoke, it was evident that he realized we weren't like the two other more demanding groups. With a smile, he continued to take our orders.

Service throughout lunch was excellent. Austin was attentive and smiley. At the end of our lunch, after all the plates were cleared, he approached me and said, "I just wanted to tell you, sir, that really meant a lot to me." Just by using his name, acknowledging him as a person, and recognizing that he had his own "stuff" going on, I had been able to shift his thinking and make a difference in his day. He and I both could have become trapped in the prejudice of previous waiter-customer relationship roles: I could have believed he was just some cranky waiter who wouldn't care about us, while he could have viewed us as a demanding group who would only find fault. Instead, by breaking out of that and reaching through to create a different relationship, I went to the human place. When was the last time you were told by a waiter that you made a difference? You can make a difference to anyone with each interaction.

I'd like you to hold a metaphorical mirror up to yourself. You know people have responded strangely to you at times. You meant one thing, but they heard it differently. So think about it ... Do you ever wake up wondering how you can do harm to someone? I hope not, and I really don't think so, since you've found your way to this chapter in this book!

Is attitude really everything? Really? Yes, it really is!

You belong in the world. And just as you deserve to be recognized for simply being in the world, so do the other beings around you. The way to notice others is to take a moment. Go beyond your schedule, you cell phone, or your contact list. Look around and become aware, mindful, and especially grateful that you can find things that really are positive in your life. Sure, you *can* fake it, but if you really think about how you approach people and if you bring appreciation to your consciousness, you can look at the world as a positive place that gives you information and other gifts you can incorporate and use.

It becomes easier to be in the world when you appreciate that the positive is there for you to enjoy. Being grateful for those positive gifts and even for the struggles lets you engage the world differently, perhaps paradoxically, and even more confidently. Don't confuse gratitude with subservience. You really do deserve to be recognized as a valuable individual.

"I'm worth being around," is a statement that's neither meek nor ego-based. This is going to take some very flexible thinking. Pause for a moment and allow yourself to link gratitude with both worthiness and confidence. Can you be grateful for all you have; feel like what you have promotes service to another person, people, or organization; and know that you are a worthy contributor? It's a pretty wonderful cycle if you allow yourself to absorb the magnitude of it.

If you show up as a contributor, as someone who is both grateful and worthy, you tend to see ego rather than display it. When you see it in someone else, it really looks pretty absurd. I fly a lot, and sometimes I get first class. When I fly, I dress comfortably. It's amusing to me to see those who have the very well-pressed designer clothes and accessories glide in front of me in line because they're first class, and by the way they look at me, I assume they've judged that I couldn't possibly be. When I stay put in line, their looks change from disdain to curiosity. I don't know their stories, and they don't know mine. That's why I don't get upset when I feel like they judge me. I don't know them, and I know they don't know me. I appreciate the absurdity. I also appreciate that we're all getting on the same plane, headed to the same location, to pick up our own very different lives. Even when I book my flights late and get stuck in the middle seat in coach, I remind myself that I and the people around me don't know each other's stories, and we're all headed somewhere. We're all worthy contributors, and we might just learn something from each other.

Attitude is the only thing we really truly have control over. Sure, the amygdala kicks in, and we get into fight-or-flight mode sometimes. Still, it's how we interpret the information in our environment that makes all the difference. Decide how to respond; don't just react. Did someone deliberately do something to you? How can you change the energy and the entire situation so that both sides feel right?

Take an inventory. As a writing exercise, take a moment and create a page or two with three columns. Don't worry; they won't be even.

In the first column, write down some of the things that can "make" you feel cranky. Really, what are your triggers to unhappiness? Some examples might include getting cut off in traffic, being accused of something you didn't do (an integrity challenge), being called a name, or being ignored or not acknowledged for the effort you gave to something.

Now, in the next column write down the sensation you have just before you begin to really get upset. What do you feel as you find your way down a path to carrying a grudge. For example, does your stomach get tight, your face flush, your jaw clench, etc.?

In the third column, write down some things you can do when you feel those trigger emotions start to rise. To summarize, what you're doing is creating a table with three columns: column 1—things that get me upset, column 2—physical signs that I'm on the road to becoming upset, and column 3—actions I can do to avert feeling upset.

This table holds significant importance. Most people know they get upset when a car cuts them off. Their response was (past tense) to blow the horn, wave a particular finger, cuss out loud (as if the other driver could hear), and maybe even chase the other driver to cut them off and teach them a lesson. See how smart that sounds as you read it? Whoa, I want that type of person around me all the time ... *not!*

So how can you feel the upset coming on, and what can you do instead? This is the value of creating a table. You're actually identifying your own triggers (of the past). As you identify them, you can let them go because you'll have a different set of resources from which to draw. You have a different state to go to because you've thought it through and you recognize that *you have choices!*

Imagine for a moment that you're driving along singing your favorite song. All of a sudden a car decides to whip around you and jam into a tiny space right in front of you. You slam on your brakes so as not to hit it. Your jaw clenches, your heart races, and you do one of the following:

1. Honk the horn

2. Wave a middle finger

3. Cuss

4. All of the above

5. Smile and blow kisses

6. Pick up a tissue and wave it at the driver with a great big smile on your face

Why would you do numbers 5 or 6? A better question than why is what happens in your body if you chose numbers 5 or 6? Can you see how both of those actions are so absurd that they might make you laugh while the person who cut you off is being oh so serious about having to be somewhere a half a minute faster than you? It's so easy to let go of the ridiculous when you make it even more absurd!

By having fun with it, you've changed your attitude. You've probably even saved your life. If getting in a car wreck didn't kill you, boosting your blood pressure would have. How great to take something ludicrous and point it out as such!

Now imagine doing that for *any* upset you have! What happens in your world? Someone demands something of you, and you feel badly that you didn't deliver it the way he or she wanted. In your head you think, *Oh, her royal highness the queen demands a redo*, and you role play. By taking it out of the realm of being so serious, you can relax and actually get your work done.

My clients know that part of my working agreements with them include comments such as *I don't take myself too seriously, though I do take my work very seriously*. That means I'll have fun getting it done. It gets done!

On a recent business trip, I found myself running to catch a plane at the airport. Certainly I could have focused on how messed up the airline was. The plane took off from San Francisco late and arrived in Chicago even later, necessitating that I hurriedly navigate my way off of the plane and through crowded concourses to catch my next flight. I could hear other passengers cursing the airline as they struggled to catch whatever connecting flight they were headed to. The absurdity of my running through an airport struck me in two ways: First, I thought, *At least I get my cardio workout in.* My second thought was, *Wow, I really love how comfortable my shoes are.*

No major airline looks at my name on a list and says, "Ha-ha! Let's make that Dr. P run through the airport today. We'll push back late as a test just for him." Airlines lose money by running late. There's no benefit in it for them at all. So when there is a problem, I shift my thinking: *I'm glad to be arriving safely rather than having that aircraft be compromised and ending up somewhere no one wanted to go that day.* And then I turn my thoughts to gratitude for the things I have like a heart that likes to beat and shoes that support me comfortably.

Sure, the delay was an inconvenience. The point is that nobody did that *to* me. Still, sometimes I come across people who seem to have gotten stuck in the "everything is going so wrong" loop. It's easy to get stuck there. It's easy to get focused on your own little world and lose big-picture perspective. A few years back, I came face-to-face with my own narrow focus. I ended up being filled with pride for my teenage son. I was in traffic, really bad traffic. I had to call my son to tell him I'd be late in seeing him. We had arranged a time and place to meet up, and there I was stuck in traffic. It wasn't just slow; it was at a standstill. I called and said that a traffic jam had occurred as a result of an accident. In fact, I reported that I had seen a life-flight helicopter land on the freeway and that it was going to be a while. His first comment was not, "Darn it. How late do you think you'll be?" What made me proud of him was that his first comment was, "Wow. I hope everybody is okay."

What a perspective! I was stuck in traffic and worried about getting to see him. He was concerned that everyone was going to be okay. It's all about perspective, isn't it?

Moving to a less life-and-death place, think about a time when you were in a restaurant or a store and saw a customer service person who had obviously had a bad day. Because she was in over her head, she couldn't see that she was perpetuating the problem by putting out such a negative vibe. By being short with customers and slamming material around, the clerk brought even more of the bad energy to herself. People approached her with armor on and defenses up, which caused a vicious cycle of the poor clerk just burying herself in bad vibes.

You might have been that employee, or you might have been the customer. Either way, you know how bad it feels. You're like a three-year-old. You just want things to go your way, and you feel like you have no control. Knowing that you can step in and actually change the course of that cycle exemplifies Choosing Your Power.

What people actually want is to be seen. I've had the most amazing service provided to me when I've approached with kindness, curiosity, and compassion, acknowledging that the other person seems to be having a hard day:

» It must be hard to work in such a rushed setting.

» You seem to be carrying the weight of your department on you today.

» It looks like it's been a hard morning for you already.

You could approach with an attitude about how terrible the interaction will be; like magic, you will get your proof. Though it would be so easy to resonate with the other person's negative energy by merely identifying that the other person is a person with human emotions, you can change attitudes. In fact, the whole interaction can change when you take control and recognize that you attract what you put into the world.

You attract what you put out there. So yes! Attitude *is* everything. When you approach your family as if they were guests in your home and offer to be more attentive and helpful and anticipate needs, you change the interactions at home. When you do the same at work, recognizing that anyone you interact with, no matter at what level, is your internal customer, you change the interactions at the office. When you approach the absurd with an attitude of making it even more absurd, you introduce an element of fun.

When you approach difficulties with an attitude of knowing that you'll get through them, somehow they become that much easier. A waiter in Jamaica gave me a great lesson on this. I had the good fortune of using my frequent flyer miles to take a trip there for my birthday. While at dinner one evening, I made several requests. I asked for more water. "No problem, sir." I asked for more bread for the table. "No problem, sir." And though I can't remember the reason, I requested a new knife. "No problem, sir."

When the waiter returned with the knife, I asked him if I might impose yet again by asking him a question. He agreed. "Every time I've asked you for something, you've responded by saying it was no problem. You smiled as you said it. Tell me, is it really always no problem for you? What happens if there *is* a problem?" His response was wonderful and a lesson that I elect to pass along to you. I've told this story many times in my seminars because it is so simple and so very powerful.

The gentleman explained to me that there really was no problem. Yes, occasionally things came up, but that would just be a situation. "You have to fix da ting," he said. He went on to explain that if you fret and worry about a situation, you still have to fix the thing that needs fixing no matter how much time and energy you've spent fretting and worrying. "So no problem. Just fix da ting, and it's no problem."

I love that! We all have choices in how we respond. Sometimes things don't go our way. So step back and find a way to make it work. No problem. Just fix the thing. And keep going ... with a smile.

Ironically, as I sit here with my final edits in front of me, my computer has gone down. I could fuss, fret, worry, or storm. None of those things would help in the production of this work. So I sit back, take inventory, do my edits and writing by hand and find work-arounds that allow me to get it done. With my EPO in mind, I find myself smiling at the opportunity to hand write this paragraph for inclusion in this book. For me, this is what Choosing Your Power is about. There are always going to be things that throw you off course. I'm grateful to have perspective and resources that allow me to recover. How about you?

With so many interactions during the day, it's essential to keep two things in mind:

1. Be grateful for the things you have that you might have ordinarily taken for granted. It will change your relationships with those things or people.

2. Recognize that you have a choice and can change your attitude at will. Let go of the notion that someone has done something to you and enjoy the fact that you get to choose how to respond. Even just recognizing you have a choice gives you power (and we'll discuss that in depth in the final chapter of this book).

Take inventory, be grateful for what you have, let go of things that aren't valuable, and fix the things you can. Follow those steps and you are actively Choosing Your Power!

CHAPTER 9

Re-Lation-Ship and the Existential Dilemma

WHO AM I IN RELATION TO?

KEY ELEMENT OF BEING HUMAN is to interact, to *be* with other people. In doing so, we act as a witness for others' lives. We watch them, we validate them, and we crave the same in return. No, not everything we do needs a parade. Still, the tasks of daily living are sweeter knowing that they matter, that as individuals our mere doing/being matters. Doing something that makes a difference for someone else gives you, as the person doing it, a reason to be. We seek to answer the existential questions of "Who am I?" and "What am I here for?" We do that by engaging with others. Again, life is about making a difference. But that then begs the question, "To whom?"

As we go from one day to the next, the power of being present becomes all the more evident. Sometimes we just "get through" this day only to come home and lavish more attention on the dog than on family members who are just as eager to see us but who have also done their best to get through their own days. Our engagement with others is not always conscious. In fact, after a while a lot of what we do becomes very "unconscious." It's not that you do what you do while knocked out; it's just that so much of the day can be done on autopilot that we miss actually being present with each other and, more important, with ourselves.

It's easy to get up in the morning and immediately assume the role we're so used to. Like putting on an old pair of jeans or sliding into comfy slippers, we just *are* who we always have been. Aren't we? Are you stuck wearing the role you've worn for as long as you can remember?

The reason you're reading this book right now really is to know that you are choosing your power and to break free from being stuck. In fact, it's an active effort to get unstuck and to consciously, deliberately get better—even if only a little—every day! Reflect for a moment. Take inventory. What roles do you play for others? Who are you in the world, and how have you let others define you? You just read that last sentence without paying attention, didn't you? This book isn't another thing to just get through. So one more time: How have you let others define you? That's a scary thought when it's put that way, isn't it? *Did you get stuck because it's really you who expects that other people expect you to be in the role you're in?* Ah, they expect it, so you have to be a mom, a student, a clerk, an assistant, a _____ (fill in the blank). Is it that you're the funny one, the emotional one, or the one who takes care of everything and everyone else? You've always been that. So you've created a track that you're doomed to stay on. Isn't there more?

Dare you even ask?

Logically you know that you are more than that role, whatever *that* role is, but you're stuck. You find it easy to be who you have been. You know you're more. What if you upset someone because they expect you to be in a particular role and you're daring to have a different emotion, thought, or reaction? You've grown, and you haven't let others see it because instead of them supporting you as the "witness" to your life, you fear they might judge you. They might judge you as being different and therefore you become afraid that you won't belong. You might be abandoned. You might no longer have them as the witness or validation in your life. So you allow yourself to stay the same, caught in a particular role. You can feel your growth stunting and your life—your life's energy—slipping away. Because it's unbearable to endure, you dull your senses to that process. TV or food or other forms of dulling self-medication become a part of your deterioration because you dare not grow. You continue on because you're expected to do just that and no more. You've trained other people to expect the constant you, and you have allowed yourself to be treated as you always have been treated because *you* fear "negative" judgment more than you fear expressing your need to grow. Ouch!

In my years as a counselor and coach, I've seen hundreds of people who live like that. That is to say, you are *not* alone. The pain you've felt, that pain you've shut off, is real. Instead of feeling growing pains, you've felt the pain of little pieces of your *self* withering away.

People stay mute because they fear they'll damage the relationships they're in. Here's what's missing in that kind of thinking: every time you've not dared to say something you know needs to be said, you've hurt yourself for the sake of sparing the other person. As a result, the relationship suffers. You haven't been honest with the other person or yourself. The relationship has to suffer. If you're not being you in the relationship, then it ends up being founded on falsehood. So where does that really leave you now?

By not saying something, you've gone along to get along. That's a reasonable strategy if it's a conscious choice you have used once or twice. When it becomes a regular pattern, you've helped create a relationship built upon lies. That becomes the antithesis—the exact opposite—of your hopes and dreams. And yet it happened ... again.

It would be easy for me to tell you to simply change how you are and you'd have a different relationship. In fact, that *is* the truth. And it is possible to create a different relationship, one that's more positively balanced.

You have to dare to BE. It takes courage to step into your true self and, on a daily basis, to consciously engage in Choosing Your Power. I'll give you a chance to look at the meaning of the word *re-lation-ship* and then to look at some of the roles people tend to wear.

You probably noticed that the title of this chapter is the word *relationship* divided up into three parts: *re-lation-ship*. It's time to test your root word knowledge. Ready? Drawing on the Latin, let's look at the meaning of the word *relationship*:

> » **Re**—here's a clue: if you redo something, you're doing it … again! So *re-* as a root of the word *relationship* means "again."

> » **Lation**—well, this is a toughie … Your clue is this graphic of gears. You see, apart they could spin independently. When they come together, they make the other gears that they touch spin with them. *Lation*, as a root word, means to come together or the way things come together.

> » **Ship**—no, in this case we're *not* talking about a big boat. The word *ship* means the state of something or, more simply, the way something

is. Consider *township*, which is the state or condition of being a town. *Stewardship* is the state or condition of being a steward or a guide for a process.

And relationship? Re-lation-ship, then, is the condition of the way things come together again. The gears in the picture are coming together to turn the other gears. People come together to engage with other people. Any time you interact with someone else, you've begun a relationship with him or her.

Do yourself a favor. Read that last line again.

Any time you interact with someone else, you've *initiated* a relationship with that other person. Not just the first time. *Any* time. The point is you are not stuck. You have an opportunity to come together again differently!

What if you've already been in a relationship with that person? What if you've been married for five or even twenty-five years? You have the power and the responsibility to change or hold that relationship. There's one thing you need to know: the other person has the same power. You can't change the other person; you can only change the relationship and the way you approach it.

A family unit, and by extrapolation a work team, behaves perfectly even if imperfect. All roles are defined. People respond to each other as they always have. No one dares to become different or stand up with a different voice. Others have described the balance of relationship as similar to that of a mobile with multiple pieces. Have you ever seen a mobile hanging in balance? Mobiles used to be popular as objects of art. Now we mostly find them hanging over babies' cribs for visual stimulation. A mobile consists of multiple objects of various shapes hanging by threads from small rods of various sizes. The dangling shapes are different sizes and positioned in different places along the various rods. It's a wonderful mixed-up assortment of shapes, sizes, lengths, and weights. The piece as a whole swings and twirls ever so slowly. And it hangs in perfect balance.

A gust of air might move this unit so it sways violently, but it will always come back to its point of balance. If you change one part on the mobile, all the other pieces will need to rearrange in order to maintain balance. Let's make this analogy a little clearer: Instead of trying to change someone else, change your own style. By changing yourself, you're automatically demanding that other styles change in response. In the example of the gears, if one of those gears grows or changes in any way, the others will move differently around it. From now on, you need to recognize the power you have. If *you* change, others will move differently around you. (Warning: you can't control *how* they change, just that they will change in their interactions with you.)

In childhood, as we grow up within families, each family member takes on a role that helps him or her get by well enough in that family. Some become dependable, some become lighthearted, some become logical, some become overbearing, and some distract from other potential dysfunction by taking on the role of the "bad" child. Each person, whether directly or indirectly, is encouraged or supported to maintain that role, and as young adults we take into the world that knowledge of what has worked up to that point. Each of us then receives feedback about the need to turn up or turn down the volume on how we play our roles. Old roles remain until we enter into a new family (such as a college clique or work group). Then we often recreate the roles we are used to. While moving away from "home" provides an opportunity to create and enact a different role, only consciously can we recognize our roles and push ourselves to become different.

Psychological and personality theorists have their own labels for people and their associated types. I won't go into details here. Instead I will offer a brief explanation of four main personality types that show up as personal styles. Do you

1. **Get It Done**

2. Do things in a **Methodical** step-by-step way

3. **Make Nice** and make sure everyone is okay and that there's no upset, or do you as

4. The **Ever Optimist** want the attention of others by showing how new opportunities can make everything better?

The **Get-It-Done** type takes on the role of making sure everything is in its place and complete. They see the end result quickly and become impatient if they're made to look at other possibilities. There are a lot of "shoulds" in this person's world. Things "should" look a certain way; they "should" be done a certain way. They don't understand why others don't think the way they do, and for better or worse, they are quick to judge. The judgment is often perceived as being accurate because it's related to the value of what the other person is offering to the conversation or relationship. That's part of what makes them so good at getting things done, though they do miss a lot of opportunities to develop a deeper relationship with the other person because they make such quick judgments. They miss that there are other people with true emotions invested in the process and who hurt when not acknowledged. On the positive side, this person's type really does know how to Get-It-Done. If you're that type, you're busy. You might want to acknowledge that others have emotions and that those emotions matter to them. That will actually help to get it done even better. If you're in a relationship with a Get-It-Done type, you'll need to speak quickly and deliver the bottom line clearly in order to be heard. You can even ask for acknowledgement; just don't over-explain why you need it.

At the other end of the spectrum is someone who may look judgmental or aloof but is simply thinking about the information before making commentary. The **Methodical** type is one who needs information, needs to compare it, and will then mull it over. Because their style is not one of making quick judgments or decisions, keep in mind that they're not being aloof or withdrawn; they're thinking. Often run over by the Get-It-Done type, the Methodical type aligns information internally and then delivers an insight that is usually brilliant. So the strength of the Methodical type is that they take information and think about it and think about it until they've reached a logical conclusion based on good evidence or information. The bad news is that they often take a long time to come out with a conclusion, however solid it is, and they appear as if they're not participating the whole time they're in the mulling-it-over stage. They might look shy or exceptionally introverted. They could in fact be great with people, though they are likely to need some time and distance from other information. If you're this type, be sure to let people know you're thinking about what they've said and give them some idea about when you'll have a comment for them. If you're in a relationship with this type, either ask for a time frame for a decision or tell them when you'll circle back to find out what their thoughts are.

The **Make-Nice** type will go out of his or her way to be sure everyone stays happy, satisfied, or at least calm. Often seen in families with an alcoholic or extremely dominant parent, the Make-Nice type has great intuition. They've had to. They needed to learn whether the key in opening the front door was an "all clear" sign or a "get ready for the storm" sign. The Make-Nice type will be the one who continues to get up from the table because *you* need something. You'll recognize this type as "the toaster" because they seem to always be popping up from the table to get someone else something, and they don't seem to ever sit down to eat or enjoy their own meals because they're giving away their peace for the sake of Make-Nice/making peace for someone else. The Make-Nice type plans events and then anticipates what will go wrong because they know something is bound to. With apologies at the ready, they enter the world armed to keep everyone happy. They're very good at it. What they don't realize is that they live life with great irony. By imposing the sense that everyone should "be happy," they do not leave room for other people to just be. In so doing, the Make-Nice type robs the other person of having his or her own experience. If this is you, you'll want to ask permission to offer help. You'll also need to practice not apologizing. Remember the chapter on permission granted? Recognize that you belong in the world and can ask for what *you* want or need. Don't give of yourself until there's nothing left. If you're in a relationship with this type of person, you can help the relationship by letting the other person know what you need from him or her (e.g. So that I can have a comfortable meal, I need for you to sit at the table with me and not continue to pop up).

Then there's the **Ever-Optimist** type. They always have stories at the ready and care deeply about being connected with other people. What makes them the optimist is that they live with a deep quest for "better." They believe *better* is available to everyone. Now. The Ever-Optimist type may drive the Get-It-Done type a little crazy. While Get-It-Done type is busy doing, the Ever-Optimist type is busy looking at alternatives and possibilities. The strength of the Ever-Optimist type is that he or she sees possibilities in almost every situation; even if they're unattainable, they're still possibilities. The weakness of the Ever-Optimist type is that in pursuing possibilities, a clear path to actual completion is clouded. Admittedly, *I used* to count myself in this group as an exclusive style. Now I call up my power and rely on fluidity to flow between each of the styles as needed. Those in the Ever-Optimist group need to acknowledge the plans of others and while appreciating their intentions also note that there are logical direct steps worth considering. Sometimes the Ever-Optimist type's offerings are seen as nothing more than a brainstorm session. Instead of a brain dump, think through some alternative paths to provide solid solutions for more realistic outcomes. We are driven by hope. Sharing that hope inspires others. If you're in a relationship with an Ever-Optimist type, then you'll need to provide clear goals and timing. If you're ever stuck, the Ever-Optimist type will have plenty of alternatives worth considering.

You probably recognized yourself in a couple of these styles. Multiple styles, or small blends of them, are possible. The idea here is that you should take the time to recognize that whatever your style, you used it *in the past* to get to where you are today. Now as an adult with your emerging power in the world and understanding that you have used a particular style and that other styles exist, *you have choices.*

The Get-It-Done type may never slow down enough to acknowledge the Make-Nice or Ever-Optimist types. If you're in the latter two groups, you may have found yourself prompted to want to give more (and actually impose more) in order to get the recognition you felt you needed. By imposing more, you've actually pushed the other person away.

Each person has his or her own space that he or she operates in. When a Make-Nice type helps to the point of taking over another person's space, it's likely that there will be some pushback from the other person. It's necessary in order for the other person to be him- or herself as a whole person. Sometimes verbally, sometimes by retreat, sometimes literally and physically, people create the space they need. This dynamic is then recreated in the next level of family, whether it's a work group or choice of partner.

Two individuals each have their own space.

As loving individuals, sometimes they overlap.

Yet when one Make-Nice type tries to over-give (yes, it is possible to over-give, essentially loving people out of the picture), then the other person becomes lost.

Feeling almost helpless, like an animal backed into a corner, he or she will become angry and lash out. When expending energy doesn't work, he or she will become withdrawn because there's no room for him or her anymore anyway. If you're over-giving, you've created this dynamic. If this person feels like there's no room for him or her, it's possible that the other person will move away, do something to get away, or hide. Essentially he or she is taking action to avoid being taken over, and he or she could literally not be there or could perhaps hide in food, drugs, alcohol, or an outside hobby because there is no longer any room for him or her.

The point again is that once you notice what you're doing, you can choose a different path. It isn't going to feel comfortable right away because it's unknown. You can do it though. And heck, it might even be fun! People change. It's why you're reading this book! The key is to become more *you* and really enjoy Choosing Your Power. And as a new, healthy, whole person, you can understand the other styles and adapt to meet each of them as needed. Sure, you'll have *your* preferences, which evolve over time as well. As long as you can be flexible in your interactions, you'll be stronger in the world.

Here's some practice for you:

1. Pick a style and be that style almost exclusively for a block of time. Let's say two hours.

2. Write down your thoughts and feelings afterward. Did others respond to you differently?

What worked for you? What felt awkward? What would you do again?

3. Repeat this with each style over the course of a few days. Step into each style and stay there for a block of time. Think that way. Interact with friends and family from that style.

4. Notice what you learned. Like writing your name with your non-dominant hand, you can do it, but it's awkward. Remember, you can choose to take on any of the traits from another style even if it's awkward at first.

Successful people know how to be flexible based on what the situation demands. Take this opportunity to practice new styles so that you have each of them at your disposal when the time is right. Sometimes you have to just get it done. Other times you'll need to think something through. There are times to smooth out ruffled feathers and other times when thinking about all that's good and possible will carry you through.

As with anything, if you do only one thing exclusively, you'll end up doing damage. Maslow, a humanistic psychologist, was famous for talking about what humans need in order to survive and truly grow. In his teaching, he said, "If the only tool you have is a hammer, you'll treat everything in life as if it were a nail." Build your toolbox by practicing something different. Trying on a different style will feel like trying on your mom or dad's coat when you were a little kid. It'll be too big and feel really uncomfortable. This feeling dissipates over time.

Now that you understand how people have grown into and use different personal styles in the world, let's reflect back on the roots of re-lation-ships and how you *come together again* with others. With new tools and new styles to practice, you've learned that you can choose to show up in the world and relate to others differently.

I've worked with a lot of business organizations over the past few decades. I've worked with individuals, couples, and families as well. Relationships deteriorate when one partner gets stuck while the other one grows. For example, it was not uncommon for me to hear, "She's not the woman I married" or "He's not the man I thought he'd become." Really? As a guy, you thought you'd get to keep a young twenty-something forever? Or as a woman, you wanted to mold him to your expectations? Surprise! He's human!

Healthy relationships have several key factors that make them work. They start with individuals who want to be better people. This is true for couples, families, or work groups. Think about yourself, how you show up, and what you're creating. For the relationship to be strong, each person wants to be whole in the world as an individual. That then allows them to join with others and create a healthy unit.

Relationships that work are founded on some key principles:

1. Each individual is a self-contained unit.

2. Each individual can share of him- or herself.

3. Each individual can *understand* the other person's point of view. Empathy is a huge success marker. Really. Not just *say* they "get it, yeah, yeah, yeah ..."

4. Each individual truly *wants* the other person to become a better individual and encourages the other person's personal growth. Note that this is not the same as encouraging professional climbing so that there's a trophy or status to hang onto. That's about personal gain. This is about allowing the other person to become bigger as a whole person in mind, body, and spirit.

5. Each individual can come together with the other person to care and share deeply.

6. By coming together, they form a unit, making up a unique individual comprised of two people.

7. Each individual can separate from that unit to become uniquely one again and willingly enter back into the two-person unit.

Think about relationships you've been in. What has been the best relationship and why? What was your part in it? Did you give? Did you take? Did you accept? Did you guide? Did you push when needed?

What might you do differently in the future? If you're in a relationship now, what can you do more of? Less of?

Have you shown that you can grow? What have you put off doing because you were too busy taking care of other people? Do you garden (even a little window sill herb garden)? Do you like photography? Painting or sculpting?

The key to a better relationship is to be more interesting the next time you come together. That is, if you are too busy trying to be a certain way for someone else, your true self can never develop or be expressed. Quit trying to make everything outside of yourself better and focus on creating the *you* that you would want to be around.

Young (immature) relationships fail because one partner doesn't feel able to express an opinion out of fear of offering the "wrong" opinion. Dare to have an opinion! The worst that can happen is that you find out you're incompatible sooner rather than later. The best that can happen is that your partner considers, appreciates, and values your opinion more and more. You'll share more. You'll ask the other person's opinion more. You'll influence each other more, and you'll *both* be growing.

This dynamic shows up at work too. Think about it. If you're at work, you're spending more of your waking hours with your work team than with your family. So how are you showing up? In what way can you push yourself to be just a little different and try on a piece of a different role for a little bit while in the work setting? Would you offer your opinion more? Speak up at meetings? And if your predominant style is the the Get-It-Done type, could you be the one *not* to speak up at meetings and instead pour everyone else a glass of water?

Do something different for yourself today. One thing. Be slightly different and see how that affects your relationships. See how it empowers *you*!

As unique individuals, we share some commonalities. Men and women tend to approach the world differently, and from a stereotypical viewpoint, that approach can be simplified. With a tip of the hat to John Gray, PhD in his work on the Mars and Venus concepts,[2] I'll take you to the very, very simple place of understanding the stereotypical: Men like parades and applause for what they *do*. Women want to be acknowledged for what they *feel*. This does not apply to all men and all women all the time, but let's start there.

Women will tell their (male) partners that they feel a certain way. Men will jump in with a "fix it" response when what's needed is a simple acknowledgement of the feeling. If you're a Get-It-Done type, you'll likely miss the feeling component of the conversation, entirely. It's necessary to acknowledge that the feeling exists in order to build and maintain rapport. Men will often report not understanding what the problem is. Their typical response is, "You said there's a problem; just do xyz, and the problem will be fixed!"

Men and women communicate differently. That's the bottom line. Women will essentially say, "I have an

2   Gray, John, *Men are from Mars, Women are from Venus*, 4th ed. Boston: Bedford/St.Martin's, (2009)

emotion. Hold it (and that's how I'll know you care)." Men respond with, "Hold it? I can do better than that! I can take it, I can fix it, and I can build it a castle!" Men go off to slay dragons, build castles, and come back for their applause and parades, all the while the women are still there, perplexed and frustrated, with their simple pleas of, "I have an emotion. Hold it."

Conflict in relationships comes from miscommunication and lack of empathy. In fact, it often stems from competition. Where men often go off to "do" for the relationship and then return for their accolades (again, you as the reader may extrapolate from the generalizations presented here), women are left to quietly "do," all the while wanting just to be acknowledged at a deeper, more emotional level.

Scorekeeping fights often result from this lack of understanding of the other's style:

"You never tell me you love me."

"Of course I do. I built that rack in the garage for you."

"Right, but you don't tell me you love me."

"You know I do. I took out the garbage."

"Well, I emptied and reloaded the dishwasher."

"Well, I mowed the lawn."

"Well, I …"

And so it goes, neither one really recognizing what the other wants. Instead of starting with "You …" start with what *you* want. In couples' communication, being able to step forward boldly and confidently, not accusingly, makes a big difference. Simply state what you want. For example, a woman could say, "Please tell me you love me. Tell me when I'm not expecting to hear it. It will let me know that you're thinking about me, and it will mean a lot to me." If we're looking at what each partner might want, the man's response could be, "When I contribute to the house, I appreciate when you acknowledge my efforts." It's important to acknowledge the request and *not* get back into the scorekeeping cycle. Even if you're feeling like you've contributed a lot more in terms of doing, reward the things you want to see more of. Then talk about it. You'll end up with good communication *and humor.* "I just did xyz!" "How nice. Shall I organize a parade, or can I just tell you I appreciate it?"

As with anything, it takes practice and work to get to where it flows easily. And it's important to explore traps along the way. Something I call catfights and pissing contests happen when territory is marked and/ or hostages are taken. We'll jump right in; your challenge is to interpret this: *Sigh, eye-roll.* "It's fine. Everything is fine." *Sigh.* Strong hostage-taking women use this tactic. The not-so-straightforward hostage takers will use the same words, but their words are swallowed in small gasps, and their eyes neither roll nor make contact with yours since they're pointed downward.

This kind of tactic might have worked before. It'll be important to move beyond it in order to build a more open communication style of stating what you truly want. Dare to speak it. When you get it, be grateful. When you don't get it, determine whether there's a communication problem, an acknowledgement problem, or an equity problem and entertain that directly.

For men, look at what territory you're marking, how far you can pee, and the so-what of it all. Step back and look at whether this situation demands that you parade your ego or whether you need to put it away and pay attention to others around you. This isn't anti-male style. It's another tool for your toolbox. Sometimes a simple acknowledgement of the other will get you much, much further along your path to a desired outcome than a competitive rant. Options and choices: All of this comes down to options and choices. The more tools you have in your toolbox, the more powerful you are as a person. We'll discuss more of that in the final chapter of this book.

Power comes from how you choose to engage with others. The *how* makes all the difference in the response you get. You can notice the response you're giving and figure out if you want to change the dynamic of the interaction as well. In the early '60s, Dr. Eric Berne did some research and developed theories about the ways people interact. In the same way I took the Mars/Venus material to its simplest level, I acknowledge Dr. Berne for his foundational work as I deconstruct it for your understanding. [3]

As we engage in the world, each of us chooses from three modes: the parent, the adult, or the child. You can watch little kids on the playground using one or another of these modes too. "Now, little dolly, you stay put until I get my juice box." That's a child acting in the parent mode. Each mode "pulls" for a specific response from the other person. We all have the capacity to enter any mode at any point.

Remember that this chapter is all about relationships. This concept will help you understand your relationships that much better. The goal of this book is for you to have as many tools in your toolbox as possible so that you have choices, not just in your understanding but in your ability to *effectively* respond. Let's say a person comes into the room and says "Why can't you just get this thing done?" It doesn't matter if the thing is a report or cleaning the whole house. In this example, someone is engaging with a level of accusation using a demanding tone. There can be one of two responses: the recipient can cower and apologize like a child who is being told he or she is bad, or the recipient can stand up like a feisty adolescent and push back. Here the first person comes in as an overbearing parent. The response being pulled for is some form of the child.

A parent style of interaction is only going to get a child style response, whether it's one of being withdrawn or one of being obstreperous. Parent pulls for child. Let's flip

3   "Detailed History and Description of Transactional Analysis.", http://www.ericberne.com/transactional_analysis_description.html

who starts the engagement. Let's say that the first person begins with a whine. "This is too harrrddd." That can be met with the response of a parent, who might retort, "It doesn't matter how hard it is. Just get it done!" Or the response could be met with another child response: "At least you have xyz tools to use. My work is hard toooo." And the whines get louder.

» A parent pulls for a child response.

» A child pulls for a parent response or a child response.

The child can also be playful. There are times when being playful is perfect. Child-to-Child makes a whole lot of sense (though that's not usually the predominant style). Playful to playful is okay...and healthy

So what style is missing? The adult style always seeks the response from the adult in the other person. This is the key to your communication and engagement with others. If you want to be heard and respected, you must enter the conversation as an adult. The good news is that because adult pulls for adult, you can change the dynamic to be just that at any point. Become conscious, and do it when you're feeling accused or like you want to hide.

Let's say you've just been met with, "Why can't you just get this thing done?" Inside you might want to hide or push back. Instead, respond with, "I'd like to talk about the expectations surrounding this project." Can you imagine the control you'll feel? The other person may attempt to stay in parent style for one or two more rounds, but he or she will eventually come to adult if you hold your ground.

If you're the one who uses parent as your style with others, look at the responses you're getting. Are people pushing back and you're not sure why? Are some hiding and frustrating you further? What would happen if you entered the conversation as an adult instead of as the parent? You might say something like, "I've noticed you haven't completed this project and wondered what it might take to get it done." Of note is that using an adult style with children actually gets a more positive response from them. You end up raising young people to be solid adults rather than raising children.

Approaching situations as the adult is straightforward and actually gets you the result you're after. Remember your EPO? Focusing on what you want brings you closer to getting it. Wow! Magic!

What about dealing with people who are just unreasonable? There are people who live in the adolescent land of getting their own ways or making everyone else's world terrible. Here I'd call on an axiom from martial arts. No, you're not going to strike back, as much as you might want to. There are two concepts to hold onto:

» Enter when pulled.

» Turn when pushed.

If someone is invested in being right, you can combat that in two effective ways and several ineffective ways.

I'll leave the latter out, since you've probably discovered many of those on your own. The concept of *enter when pulled* means that someone is so invested in being "right" that you'd only waste your energy and breath trying to convince them of your rightness. So if someone says, "The sky is purple," you can argue, or you can say, "Wow, interesting! Tell me more!" You're not saying that they're wrong, and you're not saying that you're right.

Consider a game of tug-of-war. One person wants to show how mighty he or she is, and he or she will tug. Let go of the rope or enter that person's space and watch what happens as he or she pulls. Most often, people who are used to arguing won't know what to do. You've entered when pulled, and now you have taken over the other person's center, effectively knocking them off balance.

A solid response when you have a different opinion is to state simply that. Actually giving your opinion at that point is a tactical error. Again, this is about the other person wanting to wave his or her ego around. You'll learn a lot about the person's willingness to hear versus only be heard if you make a statement of, "Oh how interesting. I have a different opinion. Tell me more." Some battles aren't worth fighting, and personally, I find that people who have made their minds up about topics such as politics or religion respond better to the enter-when-pulled strategy rather than engaging in some form of debate.

There's another notion buried in here that often gets missed. *There can be more than one right.* If you and I were to look at a cereal box, you might see a sun, a scoop, and some raisins. I'd see some kids, some writing, and a bar code. We'd be looking at the same box but seeing different things. Such is the way of the world at work or at home. People can look at the same thing and miss the other person's perspective. There can be more than one right, and dealing in absolutes is a perfect setup for failure. If you're feeling frustrated because someone doesn't understand you or your perspective, ask yourself, "What am I missing about the other person and his/her perspective?" Start there, and then go to the enter-when-pulled strategy: "Interesting. I have a different perspective. Tell me more about yours, and I'd love to share mine."

This seems so simple and so obvious. It works too! The funny thing is that people don't always use what works. They use the tools they've always used. What would happen if you started to enter when pulled? Your world would be back in your control. Hmm ... are you starting to see opportunities open up?

The second part of the martial arts axiom is *turn when pushed*. It's simple. Keep your ground without fighting about things that aren't important. Let's say you find yourself in a very, very heated argument. Cuss words are thrown at you, and you're being painted as someone completely different than who you really are. For example, no disrespect intended, if I called you "nothing but a frickin' spotted leprechaun," would you be offended? As you read that and register that its name-calling, you decide that you wouldn't be offended at being called a frickin' spotted leprechaun because it's not you;

it's an absurd thing to be called. What's the difference in being called that or some not-so-kind street expletive? Is the expletive more you, or is that just as absurd? If someone calls you a name, you either are or you aren't what you've been called, and chances are you'll know. So ... if it's not you, turn when pushed and let it slide right off of you. There's no need to waste energy and push back. It's a diversion. Stay on track with the *purpose* of the conversation. Stay "adult" and bring the conversation back to where you believe it needs to go.

In one couple's encounter, the man expressed that the woman was a terrible mother and that she always had been. She took great offense to being called such things. She recognized that the misnomer wasn't who she was. In fact, she was an excellent mother and knew it. Instead of being defensive and attacking back to defend her honor and instead of stooping to his level of adolescent mudslinging by calling him names in a return volley, she maintained control and retorted, "Interesting commentary since we're not here talking about that. Let's stay focused on ..." She won. His goal was to demean and intimidate her so that he could feel better about himself. Since she didn't take his attack personally, she won. She didn't need to do anything else except turn when pushed and essentially ignore the attack. It was a waste of energy on the other person's part. He felt embarrassed as she stayed adult and guided the conversation back its original purpose.

By seeking information and by offering to provide information, you can avoid misunderstandings and conflict. In the absence of information, people make things up. They fill in the gaps, usually with their fears and doubts. Miscommunication as the foundation of arguments starts with the lack of communication. Filling in the gaps leads to *assumptions*, and that's not healthy for individuals or those wanting to work in partnership with each other. Instead, put energy into building understanding and choose to spend time with people who want to do the same. Again, a question might arise either internally or as an inquiry of the other person: "What am I missing that is causing me to make a judgment in this way?" The other person may not know what is expected, he or she may have a limited toolbox, and he or she may be responding in the only way he or she knows how. Teach that person how to engage with you.

By becoming clear about the kind of people you want around you, you'll end up gravitating to and attracting those people. In a previous chapter we looked at envisioned positive outcomes. We explored what we wanted and specifically how to get there. Here, we look at how to reduce or even eliminate fights in relationships by focusing on what you want rather than what you see going wrong. This is about conflict resolution, and the principles will work in all of your relationships—in the office as well as at home.

Conflict and fights happen when people focus on what's wrong. The tone becomes blameful, and the response becomes defensive. Both sides go to the child mode and build resentment as each party seeks ammunition for the next sortie.

Instead, go to the adult and state what you'd like. Be specific. Begin changing the balance of the relationship by becoming much clearer in your communication. If you can do this while being loving, it's all the more powerful. Remember, you can't change another person, but you can change your approach and create conditions to allow for changes in the interaction.

Relationships are about the state of coming together again. As you come together anew, you can focus on what you want, make it clear, and ultimately create conditions to get there. You have the power to create relationships that really work well because you are consciously and deliberately Choosing Your Power!

Chapter 10

Overwhelmed by Choice

I N THE LAST CHAPTER, WE looked at relationships. The value of coming together again and both recognizing and supporting growth is invaluable in every relationship.

Independently, the pursuit of the *new* keeps us actively engaged in the world. We elect to take on more and more so that we have more to explore, more responsibility, and potentially more rewards. Ultimately we hope to be recognized or acknowledged for the work we've taken on. While we need recognition, at a more basic level we really need mental and emotional stimulation. Sometimes simply going after something new is reward in itself. Doing so fends off the boredom that comes with doing the same old thing. And as we take on more, each individual project has several uniquely assigned to-do items associated with it. And so taking on one thing usually equates to taking on half a dozen.

But we don't stop with one or two items. We say yes to more, way more. And so those "way more" items become amplified as they are each multiplied by their respective six or eight tasks. What once seemed like it might be fun becomes drudgery. And then we seek something new, compounding the tasks already before us. Unfortunately, by taking this route, we arrive at the point of feeling overwhelmed when a series of choices has led us to take on more than we can handle at any given time. Our personal resources of time, money, or energy become stretched too thin as we move into the state of feeling overwhelmed by overobligating. That is, our ambition—or worse, our desire—to please others overshadows our capacity (at that particular time). We feel like we lack the resources in that moment to handle the challenges given to us.

Realize that only the *feeling* of being overwhelmed appeared suddenly. The actual pileup and burden came to us as a result of a series of choices we made. People don't get into debt in an instant or become overweight in an instant. A series of choices led you to the point of being overwhelmed. Recognizing that can give you the perspective you need to counter the feeling of being overwhelmed. You didn't get to where you are in an instant. It will take you some time to get out of it. The most important thing to remember here is: if you find yourself in a hole, stop digging. Recognize that there are steps to take to get out from under the mounting pressure you're feeling. It will take a series of practical and different choices to come back to—and establish—a new level of operational health. Perspective is key!

The other part of feeling overwhelmed by choice is not that we've made too many choices to get us to a certain point but rather that there simply *are* too many choices to take in, sort through, and come up with the "right" solution. Being overwhelmed comes from wanting to do the right thing. We say yes to requests because it benefits us in some way. Approval is bestowed upon us in the moment of saying yes to someone's wish. And then we have to deal with the thing we've said yes to. Additionally, we worry about making the "right" decision when too many choices are put before us. So we can be overwhelmed by the choices we've made or by the choices available to us. Either way, it's an artificial pressure upon us that creates the sense of being overwhelmed.

When faced with the burdens of daily life, you might feel like you're not doing any of them particularly well. One can't simply enjoy songs like "Don't Worry, Be Happy" because life doesn't work that way. It's an easy sentiment when things are going well and flowing smoothly. Just how does that work when you've got all kinds of uncertainty about stability and a lack of clarity or direction in the personal, business, social, financial, and even spiritual parts of your life? How can we truly not worry? A few pages back, you read about a waiter in Jamaica who held the "no problem" philosophy. Yes, there are situations that need attention. The lesson was that those circumstances need attention and that spending energy worrying doesn't help. From time to time you may have a situation in which you need to "fix da ting" while recognizing that there really is no problem.

Unfortunately, our culture doesn't seem to allow that to be the norm. If you're not demonstrating outward signs of worry or feeling upset, there's a sense that whatever is going on for you must not be all that significant. As a team leader in a corporate setting a few years ago, I was called out for not being upset about a particular problem that arose. Certainly I had some concerns, so my message to my "superiors" was one of inquiry: "Would it make you feel better if I paced the floor and wrung my hands? Do I need to show outward signs of fretting, or may I sit here and more calmly create a plan of action?"

Finding a positive outcome in the midst of chaos takes concentration, relaxation, and focus. Strategic planning doesn't happen well when having to handle turmoil. Returning to your newfound skills, strive to eliminate what you don't want in order to hone in on what you do want. You'll need to keep a clear picture of your desired goal (remember the Envisioned Positive Outcome or EPO?) and then determine what steps are needed to reach that EPO. From there, the question is what resources are available to meet each of the steps needed to reach the EPO. Step back and look at how you are going to get there.

Beginning by asking *how* allows for more positive solutions to engage your thinking. Asking why something happened only serves to create a state of blame. The exceptions are in areas of engineering in which you need to backward deconstruct the situation in order to better understand the processes. Otherwise, in most businesses and relationships, the why question doesn't help. Employing a how question with a future focus allows you to arrive at an incredibly productive path toward possibility.

There are other causes that make each of us feel overwhelmed. Besides taking on too much, we might not be able to filter as well. With so much going on around us, we can be overwhelmed by our environment too. We drive, we work, we shop, and we have to deal with other people for goodness sakes! Yikes! The tool of identifying absurdity is a great place to start as you gain perspective.

Let's do a quick inventory. When you're driving, do you ever find yourself in traffic with your teeth clenched and your brow set? Do you ever feel like the tension from your back and shoulders is climbing up and nearly stopping the circulation in your neck and head? You know that feeling, and if you don't, certainly you know the kind of person I mean. They're so intent on maintaining their "superior" position in traffic that they might not let any kind of merge happen. At the very least, they need to be ahead of *you*.

If that description *is* you, then you have some work to do. Personally, I use the expressions of the other driver to remind me to check my own state of mind. When I see someone who is just cranky, I check myself. I know I don't need to match it. Sometimes just to show myself what choices I have, I go ahead and match the other person's expression. Do this: If you see someone in another car who is caught up and obviously feeling badly, try to match his or her posture and breathing. Then match his or her facial tension. No, don't mock this person; just match him or her, and you'll step into how absurd it feels. Now imagine how it would be to live that way. It's a *choice*!

Now, right now as you're reading this, do a personal inventory. Are you tense anywhere that you can let go? Do you *need* that tension? Is it serving you? (Notice I'm not saying that all tension is bad tension.) If you need it to move forward, that's fine. Paying attention helps you discern which tension is useful and which is not. You might even find tension that makes you feel a little absurd when you notice that one shoulder has climbed up by your ear. Nice posture there! The greater tension you hold, the less able you are to attract into your world the kind of people or situations you would like.

Whether it's drivers in other cars, people rushing about on the street, people in line at the coffee shop, or people fighting over a parking place, you can begin to look for the absurd. Does rushing, scowling, or barking at someone else really make for a better day? When I see someone whose shoulders are around his or her ears, not only do I wonder how he or she can hear, but I also use him or her as a reminder to check my own stress level. (What was it that Jamaican waiter said?)

As I notice those people caught up in their worlds of "should" and in such a rush, I realize that even with the burdens I'm carrying—the monthly demands and deadlines—I know that there are many people who are worse off than I am. I know that in some parts of the world the troubles I have are considered a luxury. And as I watch others wrestle with the day that has only begun and the worries they've borrowed from what lies ahead, I take a personal inventory. Dropping my shoulders, I breathe out a sigh of gratitude.

That sounds so simple, and in fact, it is. Here's the thing: you'll probably just keep reading unless I specifically ask you to *stop*. Think about what you just read.

Think of one thing for which you are truly grateful. Breathe out. Relax your shoulders. Curve the edges of your mouth into a very slight smile. Relax your eyes so they can twinkle again. Ahhh … That's better. You may want to flag this paragraph. It's one you can use in oh so many situations.

Breathing out is something you need to do so you can breathe in. Physiologically, if you were to breathe in, you could hold your breath. You could hold tension too. When breathing out, you have to really concentrate not to breathe in immediately following your exhale. In fact, when you breathe out, you then naturally breathe in. Your body requires it. If you sit calmly and breathe out, you can deliberately release the tension in your body and deliberately (on purpose, with purpose) breathe in.

To avert or overcome feeling overwhelmed, you need to know what symptoms to look for. It was once pointed out to me that every time I felt like I had too much work or there was too much stress in my life, I'd say things like, "I need a break just so I can breathe" or "I just need to come up for air." It was part of my language with other people, and I didn't even realize I was saying it at the time. Those statements have since become a flag and relaxation trigger for me. Understanding yourself enough to know when you're under stress and recognizing that you have choices about staying in stress or releasing it is a critical step in truly Choosing Your Power. You'll run your business better and become a better partner and friend.

If you find yourself overwhelmed from time to time, it's important to acknowledge it and then make a choice to do something about it. You may feel like you're in a critical downward spiral. If you were a plane, you'd need to speed up before you could pull up! As a person, you have other choices.

Just how do you keep the worry from crippling your productivity? In the next few pages, I'll give you a six-point program for overcoming the feeling of being overwhelmed. Are you ready to become "whelmed" instead of overwhelmed? Here's your six-step plan for releasing the feelings of being overwhelmed and relaxing a bit:

STEP 1: SET A STRESS THRESHOLD

The first step to feeling better and becoming better is for you to understand yourself enough to know that when you clench your jaw and tighten your shoulders, *you need to do something different.* For some people the cue is flicking a pencil. For others, it's looking into the refrigerator for the seventy-eighth time. Recognize your patterns and stress flags and *choose* to acknowledge that you are battling something that needs to be addressed. As you get better at this, it will become an automatic response. You will set a key trigger (teeth clenching, junk-food binging, etc.) that alerts you to take a deep breath. Let it out. Remind yourself about your EPO and go to step 2.

STEP 2: KNOW YOUR MONSTERS

One way to be able to relax (and even sleep) is to put onto paper all the things that are tugging at you. It's amazing how this works. Really, right now, slip away from this book (but promise me you'll come back to this page when you're done), get out paper and a pen, and just do a brain/emotion dump about all of those things—big and little—that need your attention. Whether it's a bill to be paid or a dish in the sink, if it's on your mind, dump it onto the paper.

Don't edit.

You'll prioritize later. Don't worry about listing something twice. The task is to put it all on paper, and chances are that if you find something on the list a couple of times, it's pretty significant.

The reason to do this is that it takes a lot of energy to keep minutiae—all of those small details—at ready access for your recall. Think about how a computer's RAM works; you're taxing your own system by keeping so many to-do programs running. The more things needing to be done, the more potential worry you have. In the same way that you'd put goals on paper to see them and move toward them, now put your worries on paper so that you can be clear about what's really tugging at your energy. From there you are better able to sort and prioritize. Once you shine a light on the monster in the closet, you'll see that it is more likely a shadow than a monster after all. Oh, and once on paper, it's no longer "your" monster. Might each item still need attention? Yes. And you can see, as the Jamaican waiter would explain, that you have "a situation," and really no problem.

STEP 3: CLIMB A MOUNTAIN, EAT AN ELEPHANT

Take a look at your list. Can it all be done at once? Of course not. It needs to be done sequentially; otherwise, it would already be done. As with climbing a mountain (a step at a time) or eating an elephant (not that you'd want to, but it's done a bite at a time), you'll handle your list in the same way.

You'll need a code for your triage. Drawing on my background in magic, I use a deck of cards to illustrate my example and code my to-do items according to priority:

♣ *Clubs*—place a club next to any item that needs attention but that you can get to at any point. A club item bugs you but doesn't need to be handled it right away.

♥ *Hearts*—place a heart next to any item that's relationship based. It could be a special relationship, a potential business partner, or that friend who's been on your mind and you've been meaning to contact.

♠ *Spades*—put a spade next to any item that is time critical. If you don't do this in the next three days, you could lose something big. It's okay to have another suit next to an item in addition to a spade. The spade denotes urgency.

♦ *Diamonds*—put a diamond next to any item that has the potential to boost your income. List calls to people you need to make or return, marketing steps, etc.

STEP 4: SHUFFLE AND SELECT

» Pick three. Review your list and the priorities you've put next to each, and choose the top three things you'll do today. There's still time to *do* something today. What on your list are you going to do *today*?

» Pick six. Tonight, create a list of six key items that will move you forward and get you closer to your goal. Sometimes the larger items on the list need to be broken down into smaller steps, or bites. It's okay to list those action steps. Notice I said six key items? Not ten or twelve. Six is just a bit more than a handful. It's a doable, manageable number. Handling six key items will allow you to feel a sense of accomplishment and still handle the "stuff" of the day that seems to interrupt us when we've set out on a task.

What if there are more than six items that need to be done tomorrow? The question is this: Which six are the most important? People jam their to-do lists so full that they don't get anything done. Time flies as they continue to stare at their overly full plates. If you get through all six items on your list, pick three more! Just don't stall. Keep your momentum going.

On a simple level, what I'm talking about is like picking out your clothes for the next morning the night before. If you know what you're going to wear, it makes getting up, jumping in the shower, and getting out the door so much easier. It's less to think about.

If you have a mountain in front of you and every day you have to decide which direction up the mountain you're going to head, some days get wasted because you decide not to even approach the mountain. If you've picked six items on your list and go to bed with those six things on your mind, you'll wake up with focus and determination. They're all but handled. Feeling prepared puts you at ease. When you're at ease, you accomplish more. This is the exact antidote to the crippling effects of worry and feeling overwhelmed. Hint: be sure your six items align with your EPO, or you'll find yourself under more stress doing something that doesn't serve you at all.

STEP 5: YEAH BUT TO WHAT IF

Oh, you want to play the "yeah but" game? Okay. The truth is that there will be situations you just will not know how to handle. You won't even know how to approach them. What should you do? Worry?

Sure! But why stop at worry? Let's go all out and go for panic! Try this: Put your right arm up. Put your left arm up. Wave them back and forth and yell at the top of your lungs, "Ahhh, oooo, ooohhh, nooo." Good. That was great. Now you've gotten the worry and fret and panic out of the way. Remember that thing I brought up about finding the absurd? See how good that feels?

Without going for worry or panic, what *can* you do? That's a great question, and that's just what I want you to explore! Get your paper and a pen. Choose an item (or situation) you don't know how to conquer or even get started on. Now on the page, let ideas start bubbling forth. Write down anything that comes to mind about how to resolve this particular issue. Dump it there.

Let's say you've got six bills to pay and only enough money this month to handle four of them. That's not a good place to be, but I've been there and have known enough people facing economic hardship that I can say you're not alone. Start listing all of the things that come to mind about ways to find money to cover those bills in the short term: sell something, dump out your change jar, borrow from a friend or family member, give a lesson to kids. Get creative. To paraphrase Einstein, you can't resolve a problem with the same thinking that caused it. All ideas are fair game. Don't edit; just brain dump for six minutes.

Keep the list going. Not all of them are desirable. Not all of them may be viable. The main thing is that you're retraining your thinking. The same way you study a foreign language, you can retrain your mind for possibility thinking. Instead of thinking, *Yeah but ...,* you'll begin to think, *What if ...,* and *that* is a powerful place to be. When you feel the power—*your power*—the feeling of being overwhelmed subsides.

If it feels overwhelming, you're probably asking the wrong questions. Instead of the "yeah but" catastrophe thinking, substitute what or how questions focusing on the outcome you want (your EPO), and you'll be able to celebrate how you actually take on the habit of choosing your power. Watch yourself! Catch yourself. It takes practice!

STEP 6: KEY STRATEGY— REMEMBER YOU HAVE A CHOICE

Setting your plan for tomorrow is an excellent way to create a strategic action plan for yourself. Once you're good at the tomorrow thing, then (and only then) you can begin to extrapolate out for the week and maybe even the month. What you need to know is that no matter what, as long as you're still aboveground (that is, you're not dead), you have a choice.

The action associated with this step is simple. Ask yourself this question: "What is available to me right now?" Again. "What is available to me, right now?" And then ask, "What choices can I make?" Asking these questions will remind you that you actually have a choice, and it alerts your mind to seek answers not readily apparent. When you ask, "What's available to me right now?" and then ask it a second or third time, you're training your mind to recognize that each moment is different and that new awareness brings new choice. (More about that concept shortly.)

Seeing what was previously unseen puts you back in control by going through the steps of feeling overwhelmed, containing it, recognizing the absurdity of certain responses, and ultimately feeling confident that the right choice will emerge. Having a strategy for dealing with feeling overwhelmed and asking the right questions puts you in a different mindset. Once you feel back in control, you can deal with the situation. As my waiter reminded me, "No problem!"

Choosing Your Power implies just that: the power to choose. So do that. Choose. Course correct if you have to, but don't stall out. You have power and confidence that come from knowing that in making a decision, you cut off the other intrusions. The word *decide* comes from the Latin meaning "to cut off," and that's important when faced with an overwhelming amount of choices. Decide— cut off other choices—and boldly move forward.

You have choices. Just knowing that gives you power. Managing your choices gives you focused direction. The next chapter delves into how to create true power and freedom as you continue forward on your journey of Choosing Your Power.

CHAPTER 11

Spiraling Toward Freedom

FIRST ROOTS, THEN WINGS—IT'S WHAT we all need ... all we crave, really. We each need something we can believe in and that grounds us. Then we need the ability to fly, to try out the new, to explore and grow, all the while building on the roots that allowed for our growth.

In this journey we're on, you've become conscious of taking steps to become actively engaged in Choosing Your Power. By now you're getting it. It's sinking in, and you've gained new tools you might already be using. You know where you've been, and you have a clearer idea of where you're heading. You know what you don't want, and that gives you better direction about what you do want. You also know that it's easy to revert back to your old ways. Of course, doing so means that the results you get will be the ones you've always gotten. Your past gave you some solid experiences. You've learned from them. Don't shut them away; reflect and build on what you've learned. Very likely, the lesson is that you're stronger than you thought you were. Aren't you ready for some new experiences now? Oh yes. Yes, you are!

Look more closely at your foundation, and you'll see that you have had strength all along. Sometimes I feel like the Wizard of Oz when I point those things out to people: "Hey, Cowardly Lion, you have the courage you need. Just look at the adventures you've been on so far. You've survived quite well, haven't you?" Take inventory. Something has gotten you to this point, right? You could have crumbled, and maybe you did to some extent at one time or another. Still, you had the fortitude to pick up this book. That in itself is strength. The desire to learn, grow, and become powerful is one thing. To actually do something about it and push yourself to learn and grow and to actively, honestly, and deliberately step into Choosing Your Power is something else!

It takes fortitude to actively choose. What gives you that strength? Something inside you, consciously or subconsciously, has led you to where you are now. Really, you have given yourself the strength. This book is about building on the tools you have, giving you new tools, and making it all *consciously* driven. Think about being in the process of moving from desire to destination. That process actually gives you some form of stability, whether or not you currently feel fully stable. Recognize that having a broader menu of survival and growth tools from which to choose gives you the breadth and depth to become very, very solid in yourself. You have some tools; now use them correctly and don't, for example, use them to hide. You're continually building other tools and skills; keep building!

All of your past experiences have given you a foundation upon which to build your future. Can you recognize that they don't define your future? The roots you establish, the roots hold you deeply and firmly, create the support you need to launch yourself forward; they don't hold you hostage to your past. Yes, you always have that foundation to come back to. That sense of strength becomes a part of you. Still, to raise yourself beyond your foundation you also need wings. You *need* to fly.

Your growth as an individual requires that you not simply stay rooted but that you expand, explore, and embrace new territories—thoughts, concepts, and ways of being—that you haven't yet encountered. Welcoming the new means being open and vulnerable to the uncomfortable. By engaging in the practice of taking on new skills, you prove to yourself and others that you have wings. Becoming comfortable with what was once new gives you deeper, broader roots. And again, use your roots as a launching point. Do both consciously; be aware of the roots you're currently establishing and watch yourself as you push into your personal discomfort zone and decide to fly anyway.

You know that each of the tools you've learned about will help you be more solid in the world. What you may not have worked on yet is the reason for doing all of this. What comes to mind when you think about the need or strong desire to grow? What are you becoming, and what are you moving away from being? Both of those questions help establish the reason for growth.

In chapter 7 covering what I call Wayne's Watch Words, you learned not to ask others the question why unless you're a scientist and really have to backward engineer a problem. You're about to get permission to bend that rule and make it a guideline. Yes, you can ask why of yourself in this situation. In fact, here's your next exercise as you wrap up this final chapter and get ready to head into the world: Why does it matter to you to grow from where you've been?

Honestly, it's really important that you dig out the true nature of your purpose. You may come to an answer quickly, or you may deliberate on it for a while. Don't ask anyone else. This is *all* you!

Why does it matter to you to grow from where you've been?

From there, from whatever answer pops up for you, I want you to ask another question of yourself: Why? That's right, another one! It's important to ask yourself the purpose behind the purpose, and once you have that answer, do it two more times. Each time you'll be further exploring your purpose by asking yourself, "And why is *that* important?"

Psssssst! Stop reading for a second and get your journal, use the workbook included at the end of this book, or download the workbook pages for free at www.

ChoosingYourPower.com. Getting to your purpose as you progress on your journey clears the way to choose *your* path.

So now that you've asked yourself why it matters to you to grow from where you've been, and you've asked yourself why that answer is important to you at least three more times, it means you have permission to ask the why question four times total. What did you learn?

As important as the answer is, the process and what surfaces *with* the answer is just as important, if not more so. If you don't have a journal by this point, you really do need one. It's different to handwrite your thoughts than it is to type them. Write. Take some time to explore. Write whatever comes up. This is really where your roots and wings begin to take shape. You're determining what you value the most by exploring *your* reasons to grow.

More than likely you're pushing yourself to grow because of some injustice in the past. You're moving away from something you have been dragging along for a long time. You're righting a wrong, and you're eager to enjoy all of who you can become by actively Choosing Your Power. It's an exceptionally noble endeavor and certainly beats the alternative, which is doing nothing.

Finding your true purpose matters. The reason you're doing any of this work is fundamental to who you are and what you'll end up giving back to the world. Reflect on what you learned in chapter 8 on Attitude and Gratitude. It's about showing up and giving. By enduring struggle, you take on a perspective that allows you to give what's needed. There's truth in the concept that the wounded healer best knows truly how to heal. Your gift to yourself and others is in your recovery. What did you learn as you carried the emotional and sometimes physical scars from the past? What did you incorporate into who you are? What emotional overlay can you let go of so that you can more fully use the gift of experience? What can you share with others to help them, to make it about them, and to stop needing or demanding that others pity you for your story?

This is strength. You *get* to choose to acknowledge your history, to stop being weighed down by the memories of misfortune, and to take on the possibilities of the new while sharing your knowledge and your strength. Power comes from learning from your roots, believing in your wings, and recognizing the purpose that drives you.

As a person with purpose, you're constantly faced with choices in the world. Having roots doesn't mean staying rooted and getting stuck again. It means having the strength to be solid. Having wings doesn't mean flying off in any direction; it means being driven by a purpose and exploring how to best help others see, hear, and engage with you while you stay focused on *your* purpose.

Your purpose defines your day, how you plan your schedule, how you prioritize the action items—your to-do list—and acts as the filter for whether something belongs in your world right now or needs to be put on the "maybe someday" list. When most people find their true purpose, they recognize that it involves interacting with or giving to others. One's purpose often focuses on helping other people. The caution here is that you not fall back into old patterns of giving your *self* away as you give to others. Explore what it means to you to give to others. Does it really matter if you show up and offer your experience from the place of your own personal wounds? It does. Your purpose ties to your personal power. In the process of healing, you can give to others. You're continuing on your journey and exploring tools that work for you. Everything you're learning and have adapted from previous chapters is yours to use at any point from now into the future.

What are you choosing to focus on? If you focus on where you were stuck, you'll stay stuck. The worthy struggle of the human condition is to keep going. Focus on the strengths you've developed that have kept you moving forward. In this the final chapter of this book, reflect on the walls that had penned you in so that you can instantly knock them down when they arise again. Will you need to look at what you don't have in order to focus on what you want, moving yourself from desire to destination? Sure! Just don't live in that space of lack or what's missing. The truth is that you've been stuck because you *only* lacked the ability to see beyond the boundaries you had in place. That's not a blameful statement as much as an assessment of your recent state. Those boundaries were useful to keep your world stable. But that's not the reason you chose to pick up this book and read this far. You got tired of what was. You needed to move to something new, and as scary as it is to think about moving to that place of new, you're making it happen. You can't read these words, think about what is possible, and then return to what was without becoming depressed. You can choose to regress, but that's not why you're here, is it? You have a purpose, so break out of what was and move forward to what is becoming!

Take inventory. Really. Look back at times you've felt stuck.

Think about what you did, what you saw, what rang true for you, or what deeply moved you to a new state of awareness. What shifted your perception? Something happened, and when it did, you *knew* you had to do something different. It could have been that the situation got worse. It could have been that a new opportunity arose that you hadn't seen before. Was it new, or had it been there all along?

There's a theory that has held my attention and interest ever since I first learned of it. It's a special branch of philosophy and theology called hermeneutics. Very simply put, hermeneutics is a branch of philosophy that focuses on looking at the way things are interpreted. It's a methodology of looking at a person's understanding and values at any given point in time. For example, ancient texts are interpreted based on the understanding of the time in which they were written. Looking at 1950s television today and pretending the messages are current would be fallacy. Looking at ancient texts and ignoring the context in which they were written would be worse.

So why go into that here? Because it's the foundation for your freedom. You see, it's all about the context in which you understand something and the perspective you hold when you examine that something.

What is your understanding of anything before you explore it? What changes once you've explored it? Do you change? Does the thing you've explored change? Do you acquire new knowledge or adapt knowledge you already had? Do you become stronger in the beliefs you had prior to the exploration, or do you gain an even broader perspective and perhaps a desire to explore further? Think about the evolution of your roots, your wings, and your purpose. They haven't always been the way they are now, and that is a good thing!

Hermeneutics, as a particularly specialized field of philosophy, has at its core a basic circular concept. Namely, *to know I must understand, and to understand I must know.*

UNDERSTANDING LEADS TO KNOWLEDGE, WHICH LEADS BACK TO UNDERSTANDING

What that means for you in the "real" world about getting unstuck is this: if you think about that circular concept, you'll recognize that you only have the ability to interpret based on your understanding of a certain situation. That means if you're stuck and you know you're stuck, you need to look for another perspective into your situation and use different thinking processes other than the ones that brought you to where you are.

How do you find that alternate perspective?

1. Recognize that you need a different perspective.

2. Ask the right question. For example, what's available to me now ... and now ... and now?

Asking that question reinforces the notion that you actually have a Choice. When you have a Choice, you are—by definition—no longer stuck! So create a new circle and recognize that Awareness leads to Choice, and Choice leads to new Awareness.

Awareness leads to Choice

Choice leads to Awareness

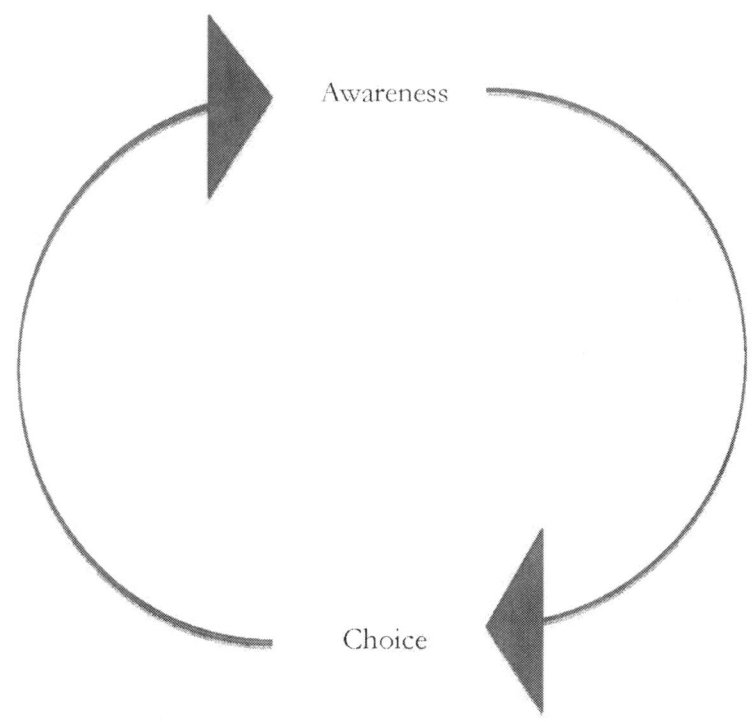

As my Awareness grows, I see I have more Choices

As I see my Choices, I have a new Awareness

This variation on the hermeneutic circle mandates personal growth. You cannot have awareness and choice and stay stuck. By this point in your learning, you now know that if you stay stuck, it's only because you've made a conscious choice to do so. So in effect, you've made a choice and ... oh, you have awareness about doing so. You've expanded. Surprise! See how that works? If you become aware that you're stuck, you can ask the questions of what's available in that moment and recognize that each moment brings the potential for new awareness. That again brings you back to choosing, deliberately!

The most interesting thing about this circle, or cycle, is that it isn't really a circle at all. In fact, there's no way that with a growing awareness you could ever come back to *exactly* the same place where you were. That is, unless you actually *choose* to. And then you're not stuck, you're just choosing, willfully and deliberately choosing to take action or engage in inaction. If you choose the latter, it is most likely based on fear. We'll explore that shortly. For now, let's look at what it means to stretch your awareness and realize that you have this gift of choice!

The gift of choice means you can't stay stuck. You simply cannot come full circle and arrive back where you started in your thinking, though you can pretend and choose to show up no differently in your way of being. Still, your thinking will have changed, and you will know that you're really lying to yourself. Ahh, there's something you're reflecting on now that has you wondering if maybe you've been lying. Sorry. It's likely that if you're wondering, you're only trying to continue a lie that hurts. Look back and then look at your current situation. You're not really protecting anyone, are you?

In terms of the circle of thought where awareness leads to choice, if you started at the bottom and you came around to the same place, because you've been expanded by a new awareness of choice, you *can't* end at the same place. You've been elevated to the next level. You could recognize that if you have this choice, there may be more; and with a new awareness, you can gain a new perspective, coming up one more level and looking at alternatives to your situation differently. Keep asking the right question, and you'll continue to get new answers.

What's available to me *now*—with every breath—implies that there is something new available. Look at yourself and your situation and recognize that each moment gives you the possibility of new understanding. You will at some point look back and realize you never *needed* to be stuck. Some people get depressed when they realize they've "wasted" time being stuck. The point is not to wallow in what was or what could have been. The point is to expand your current thinking, learn from the past, and grow further. In fact, when you take this approach it's possible that you may even experience some elevation of spirit in this upward spiraling path toward freedom. With new awareness, new choices come. When you recognize that the spiral is endless, you may find yourself connecting with the infinite.

As you read this, do you find yourself breathing differently than when you first started this chapter? Do you have a sense of possibility? Or did you let the committee in your head take over and lead you to become frustrated that you don't have *the* clear path laid out for you? That might lead you to flogging yourself by telling yourself you "should have" and "could have" done all this sooner. Now you have to decide if that kind of thinking is useful because of all that is possible to experience. It's even possible to experience it all at once. Odd, isn't it? Next look back at that "stuck" place, take inventory of what you're feeling right now, and ask yourself, "What's available to me now?" Smile and breathe as you ask yourself that question this time.

Asking yourself what is available to you now presupposes that options not only exist but continue to be there for you. That becomes a welcome opportunity *and* an awesome burden. If you have choices, you *must* take action, because now inaction has become an active choice.

Sometimes people choose to shut down because they're afraid. Being anxious about the unknown is often interpreted internally as fear. When people don't know what to expect, they enjoy a dance between anxiety and excitement. Choose to interpret your experience as excitement and then deliberately pay attention to what you're choosing to pay attention to. That is, don't create a problem by seeing a problem.

What? Another circle? No, not really. This time it's more like a little bump in the road. It's easy enough to get over. Sometimes people are afraid to look inwardly at what they're feeling, and sometimes people are afraid to take action because they don't know the "right" direction. Remember that in chapter 5, we explored the concept of taking action and course correcting from there. Make a decision, head in a direction, explore new territory, and you'll find that once your perspective is stretched, you can never go back to your original perspective.

You're aware of new options, and you're *choosing* action as you engage in making new choices. Celebrate! As noted earlier, this is a reminder to applaud yourself for your successful efforts as you make new choices and take on new responsibilities.

Then take action. With your new set of skills, what do you really want to do now?

Write it down.

Plan your next steps.

Take action, keep your EPO in mind (remember chapter 6), and ask two key questions:

1. How is what I'm doing getting me closer to my Envisioned Positive Outcome?

2. What's available to me now? (Awareness leads to Choice; Choice leads to new Awareness.)

With each step, you are on an expanding path of bettering yourself. Look at where you've been. Look at where you are now.

As you move forward, keep in mind that for every step you take, you're making a difference—a difference to yourself—and in so doing, you're making a difference to those around you. By bettering yourself, you're enhancing the lives of others and bringing rewards to yourself. Every morning you can awaken anticipating the steps you need to take to get you closer to your EPO. You'll smile with the promise of opportunity as your feet hit the floor.

I think about the lessons I learned from my dad when my own feet hit the floor each morning, and I'm filled with possibilities. My dad often closes phone conversations with, "Do good stuff!" I'd invite you to take his advice as well, and as you review the messages in this book, you'll find that you can learn a little more with each pass while focusing on the "good stuff" you can do for others and yourself.

That's the exciting part of this journey. It's *your* journey. You get to decide what you will work on for yourself first. This journey allows you to continue to spiral upward—not circle back. You're on your way to true freedom as you gain the deep knowledge that Awareness leads to Choice and that Choice *is* freedom.

That knowledge, that Awareness, that Choice is yours in each moment. Stay aware, seek possibilities, and take action. That is your key to freedom and your ability to become and express more of who you really are. You've embarked on a remarkable journey—*your* journey. Thank you for letting me be a part of you becoming the amazing person you can and deserve to be. In every moment of every day, remember who you are. Remember who you deserve to be and how you can be seen, heard, and recognized in the world. Work on bringing to yourself more of what you truly desire and stay focused on what you have. I know you will create a wonderful world of amazing possibilities and positive outcomes as you continue **Choosing Your Power**.

REFERENCES

Mehrabian, A., *Silent Messages: Implicit Communication of Emotions and Attitudes*, Belmont CA: Wadsworth (1981) (currently distributed by Albert Mehrabian, am@kaaj.com)

Gray, John, *Men are from Mars, Women are from Venus*, 4th ed. Boston: Bedford/St.Martin's, (2009)

"Detailed History and Description of Transactional Analysis.", http://www.ericberne.com/transactional_analysis_description.html

CHOOSING YOUR POWER
Workbook
Action pages to help you in Choosing Your Power

The following pages will help you track your work from ideas sparked throughout the **Choosing Your Power** book.

Please let me know how you are doing on your journey by posting on my Facebook page at www.Facebook.com/ WaynePernell

You can also download this workbook and other great content for free while learning about new offerings at www.ChoosingYourPower.com

All the best to you as you continue engaging in
Choosing Your Power!

www.WaynePernell.com   www.ChoosingYourPower.com

Wayne • Pernell

CHOOSING YOUR POWER
Workbook
Action pages to help you in Choosing Your Power

WANT VS. NEED –

What do you **NEED**?

What do you really really **WANT**?

- » I want (financial)

- » I want (social – including family & friends)

- » I want (spiritual)

- » I want (physical)

- » I want (community)

Take a moment to explore these and complete the above sentence starters here. Getting clear helps set a truly positive direction.

© 2012 Wayne D Pernell

www.WaynePernell.com   www.ChoosingYourPower.com

CHOOSING YOUR POWER
Workbook
Action pages to help you in Choosing Your Power

Stay neutral for now –

Describe what you're wearing:

www.WaynePernell.com   www.ChoosingYourPower.com

CHOOSING YOUR POWER
Workbook
Action pages to help you in Choosing Your Power

Describe your surroundings – stay neutral – go!

Now, using what you wrote on the previous page, go to a place of identifying something nice about yourself. This is practice. Physically doing the exercise is different than just reading it, saying "Oh, I get it," and dismissing it.

For now, focus on your clothes; then focus on your environment. After that, you can focus on your job, your family, your car, your friends, etc.

Ready? Go!

© 2012 Wayne D Pernell

www.WaynePernell.com   www.ChoosingYourPower.com

CHOOSING YOUR POWER
Workbook
Action pages to help you in Choosing Your Power

The things that "make" me cranky are:

The sensation I get when I start to feel upset is:

The things I can do to when those trigger feelings show up are:

www.WaynePernell.com   www.ChoosingYourPower.com

Wayne • Pernell

CHOOSING YOUR POWER
Workbook
Action pages to help you in Choosing Your Power

STYLE PRACTICE –

Which style are you?

Which style did you choose to be for two hours?

What worked?

What didn't work?

Did others respond to you differently?

What did you learn?

What about that style would you choose to adopt and practice until it's comfortable?

© 2012 Wayne D Pernell

www.WaynePernell.com   www.ChoosingYourPower.com

CHOOSING YOUR POWER
Workbook
Action pages to help you in Choosing Your Power

KNOW YOUR MONSTERS

(Oh, and once written, they're no longer "yours" to keep. That's the point!)

Brain Dump: Write down ALL of the things that are on your "should" list – the gotta get done – the nags and tugs at your time, attention, and energy. You'll prioritize later. For now, brain dump here!

www.WaynePernell.com   www.ChoosingYourPower.com

CHOOSING YOUR POWER
Workbook
Action pages to help you in Choosing Your Power

BRAINSTORM ACTION STEPS:

Pick an item that needs to be handled. Write it down as a specific question – "How do I cover all of the bills this month?"

Give six minutes of attention to that question, writing down *all* of the ideas that come forth. You'll decide what's viable later.

Ready? Write your specific question.

Go!

www.WaynePernell.com   www.ChoosingYourPower.com

CHOOSING YOUR POWER
Workbook
Action pages to help you in Choosing Your Power

Know Your Purpose – Choose Your Path

Answer the following and then explore "why" four times. Yes, here – for your self exploration – you may use the word "why" to uncover the real reason you're heading down a particular path. Why does what you're doing matter?

*Why does it matter to you to grow
from where you've been?*

www.WaynePernell.com   www.ChoosingYourPower.com

And why?

And why?

And why?

And why?

So, what is your purpose?

Live It!

And Continue **Choosing Your Power**!!!

www.WaynePernell.com   www.ChoosingYourPower.com

About the Author

Sharp, insightful, witty, and playful, Dr. Wayne Pernell brings more than thirty years of experience in human potential enhancement to his writing and coaching. Having worked with individuals, couples, families, corporations, and organizational work teams, Wayne knows the power of the envisioned positive outcome.

Wayne, a native of California, grew up on the beautiful Palos Verdes Peninsula grateful and inspired as each day was punctuated by a magnificent sunset over the water. Encouraged to explore topics about which he was curious, he began studying hypnosis at the age of twelve. He knew he had found his calling as he understood deeply that *what the mind can conceive, the body can achieve*. Wayne's father, a dentist and entrepreneur, encouraged his academic pursuits. His mother balanced the humanistic aspects of his world by supporting his passion to enter the field of psychology and contribute to the arenas of human potential enhancement and transformational leadership.

After earning his doctorate in clinical psychology, Dr. Pernell's career path took a fairly atypical route; rather than setting up a private practice to see individuals and couples, he worked with leaders in organizations and found that line staff became appreciative of the opening communication pathways. By building bridges between line staff and leadership, organizational efficiency ensued. Dr. Pernell's work has included leadership coaching within such companies as Schwab, 3Com, Whole Foods Market, and AAA. In addition, Wayne developed a solid business background in the service industry by heading a locked psychiatric facility for five and a half years. He also briefly consulted in the role of interim director at the Haight Ashbury Free Medical Clinic in San Francisco. Dr. Pernell has enjoyed the last several years as a senior consultant and organization development executive at the Pride Institute, helping dental practices get better at what they do by providing proven systems and building skillsets for all team members.

Throughout his journey, Dr. Wayne Pernell has continued coaching individuals and consulting with organizations, always looking for ways to help people support each other. Bettering each other as individuals helps better the community as a whole.

As a fourth-degree black belt, coach, and author, his influence spread to the community. As Sensei Wayne, he taught students to continually assess what options are available so that conflict can be minimized or eliminated. Drawing on concepts from Bushido (the "Way of the Warrior"), Sensei Wayne helps his clients (and his readers) get through tough spots and reduce conflict in their lives by emphasizing the power of choice even during extremely high-pressure situations.

Also known as "Dr. Wayne" or "Dr. P," this man of many skills is no stranger to the stage. In addition to coaching individuals and organizations, speaking, and training groups of all sizes internationally, Dr. Pernell is an accomplished magician, having performed locally and across the world to the amazement and delight of a wide variety of audiences.

When not on the road, Wayne is happily at home in Northern California just south of Napa Valley in his blended family with his wife, two sons (now off to college), daughter, and two bonus daughters (not to mention the two cats and fish).

To receive tips and updates from the author, please find him online at www.Facebook.com/WaynePernell and be sure to see what's new for you at www. ChoosingYourPower.com.

Keep moving forward and enjoy the challenge and the rewards that come from **Choosing Your Power!**

CPSIA information can be obtained at www.ICGtesting.com
Printed in the USA
BVOW031445010213

312182BV00001B/52/P